A
GOURMET'S
GUIDE TO

VEGETABLES

A GOURMET'S GUIDE TO

VEGETABLES

LOUISE STEELE

Photography by
DAVID GILL

HPBooks
a division of
PRICE STERN SLOAN
Los Angeles

ANOTHER BEST SELLING VOLUME FROM HPBOOKS

Published by HPBooks
A division of Price Stern Sloan, Inc.
360 North La Cienega Boulevard
Los Angeles, California 90048

9 8 7 6 5 4 3 2 1

By arrangement with Salamander Books Ltd. and Merehurst Press,
London.

This book was created by Merehurst Limited
Ferry House, 51/57 Lacy Road, Putney, London, SW15 1PR

Photographer: David Gill
Food Stylist: Maria Kelly
Home Economist: Maxine Clark
Assistant Home Economist: Jacqueline Clark
Color separation: Kentscan Limited
Printed in Belgium by Proost Internationl Book Production, Turnhout

Library of Congress Cataloging-in-Publication Data

Steele, Louise, 1945-
    A gourmet's guide to vegetables.

    1. Cookery (Vegetables) 2. Vegetables I. Title.
II. Title: Vegetables.
TX801.S73   1990   641.6'5   89-26758
ISBN: 0-89586-847-4

Contents

Introduction

Try to imagine a world without vegetables—it's a bleak thought! Fortunately, instead we are almost spoiled with a glorious range of delicious vegetables. Never before has such a variety been available in supermarkets and produce markets.

Vegetables come in a dazzling array of colors and shapes, with wonderful flavors and textures—some more familiar to us than others. *A Gourmet's Guide to Vegetables* aims to help you make the most of them, with practical advice on when to buy and what to look for, plus plenty of information on preparation and cooking, imaginative serving suggestions and a feast of beautifully illustrated step-by-step recipes.

The vegetables have been grouped according to type: brassicas, root vegetables, onions, peas and beans, stalks and stems, fruiting vegetables and so on. Each section is illustrated with color photographs to make the less familiar ones easy to identify.

The recipe section includes ideas for soups and starters, main courses, accompaniments and salads, plus a selection of vegetarian main courses. Some ideas will, hopefully, inspire you—some may even surprise you! Suggestions range from Spiced Pumpkin Soup and Filo-Wrapped Vegetables to Sorrel & Asparagus Crepes and Cucumber & Strawberry Salad.

Whether you would like to experiment with unfamiliar vegetables or simply add to your own repertoire of vegetables dishes, you will surely find plenty of ideas here to grace any table and delight the gourmet palate.

Cabbage

The cabbage (*Brassica oleracea* var. *capitata*) is said to have originated in the eastern Mediterranean and Asia Minor. This indispensable, though much maligned, vegetable has changed a lot through the centuries, and it was not until the 16th century that the firm-headed types appeared.

There are many different varieties available throughout the year: green, white and red. They may be round or conical, tightly-packed or loose-leaved or smooth or curly. Green cabbages are the most widely grown and are around all year.

Spring cabbage, in season from winter through to spring, is a young cabbage harvested when the heart is only partially developed. It has smooth dark-green leaves, which are loose or small-hearted.

Spring greens are small, young, mid-green, leafy cabbages, sold before the hearts have developed.

Savoy cabbage—considered to be one of the best for flavor—is the pretty one with crisp, curling outer leaves and a firm green head. It is available from late summer.

White cabbage has a firm, hard crisp head with smooth leaves and is available for most of the year.

Red cabbage is in season from spring until mid-winter. It is hard, tightly-packed, crisp and dark red or crimson.

Bok choy from China, also known as Chinese cabbage or Chinese chard, is a slender type of cabbage with broad green leaves, tapering to crisp white stalks. It is similar in appearance to Swiss chard and should not be confused with Napa cabbage, which are white and crisp, see page 12. It is available from Chinese supermarkets and some produce markets. It is usually served stir-fried, although it may be prepared and served in the same way as other types of cabbage.

Buying & Storing

Choose fresh-looking cabbages with compact heads. A good quality cabbage should weigh heavy in the hand. It is best to use cabbage as soon as possible after buying or harvesting, although the hard varieties keep well for a week or more in a cool place. Store the more leafy varieties in a plastic bag in the crisper drawer of the refrigerator up to two days.

Preparation & Cooking

Discard coarse outer leaves and wash the cabbage thoroughly. Cut hard types in halves or quarters for easy handling. Cut away the center stalk, then shred, cut in wedges or leave whole, depending on how the cabbage is to be used.

Cabbage is all too often ruined by overcooking. It should be cooked only until tender-crisp to enjoy its flavor and texture; overcooking also deprives this vegetable of its nutritional content. Steam or boil in a very small amount of salted water or chicken stock until just tender: five to seven minutes for shredded cabbage; about 12 minutes for wedges or quarters. Always drain well before serving.

Serving Suggestions

The hard red and white types are delicious shredded raw into salads: try a mixture of the two with bean sprouts and green bell pepper, dressed in a ginger vinaigrette.

Red cabbage is most often used either in pickling or for long, slow cooking in braises and casseroles; it is excellent with rich meats such as venison, duckling and sausages.

The hard white type, cut in wedges, makes a lovely addition to casseroles or pot roasts and chunky soups in the French style.

Use blanched cabbage leaves (Savoy is perfect) to enclose meat and rice fillings for tasty variations on the Greek Dolmades theme.

Try cabbage Chinese-style: stir-fried it retains its color and crispness. Boy choy is particularly good cooked this way: coarsely shred the leaves and stalks crosswise before stir-frying. Cook well-dried finely shredded green cabbage oriental-style: deep-fry until crisp and use in Chinese dishes.

Savoy cabbage

Spring cabbage

Miniature red cabbage

Red cabbage

White cabbage

Spring greens

Brussels sprouts

Brussels Sprout

Brussels sprouts *(Brassica oleracea* var. *bullata gemmifera)* were first grown in Brussels as long ago as the 13th century. These vegetables, like miniature, tight-headed cabbages, belong to the Brassica family and are in season during autumn and winter. Their flavor is said to be improved by a touch of frost.

Buying & Storing
Look for small, firm, fresh green sprouts. They will keep well up to two days, stored loosely in a plastic bag in the crisper drawer of the refrigerator.

Preparation & Cooking
Wash just before cooking, remove any loose outer leaves and trim stem end (not too close or sprouts will fall apart during cooking). Cut a cross in the bottoms of the stalks for even cooking of the sprouts.

Do take care when cooking — sprouts really are most unpleasant if overcooked (as they all too often are!) Bring a pan of salted water to a boil. Add sprouts, cover and cook at a full rolling boil six to eight minutes (depending on size), until only just tender and still bright green in color. They may also be steamed (in which case allow a few extra minutes cooking time), or braised in a little butter and chicken stock. Drain Brussels sprouts well before serving.

Serving Suggestions
When at their peak, young and tender sprouts are delicious finely shredded and served raw in winter salads or added to stir-fry dishes. Brussels sprouts with chestnuts are traditionally served with Christmas turkey, and are a good accompaniment at other times; use canned chestnuts when fresh are unavailable.

Sprouts are also delicious served tossed in melted butter with a sprinkling of crisp, crumbled bacon and tiny garlic croutons. Sprouts pureed with butter, cream, mashed potatoes and a little nutmeg make a dish that's both colorful and tasty. Try them pureed in a cream soup, garnished with puff pastry and a sprinkling of Emmenthaler cheese.

Kohlrabi

Despite its rather strange appearance, kohlrabi *(Brassica oleracea caulorapa* var. *gaugyloides)* is a member of the cabbage family. It is believed to have originated in the East and is particularly popular in European countries and the Orient. It has a round swollen green or purple stem bottom, from which leaf stems grow.

Buying & Storing
Kohlrabi is available from summer until early winter. Select firm small bulbs, ideally no larger than a tennis ball—any bigger and they tend to be coarse-textured. They will keep in the crisper drawer of the refrigerator up to three days.

Preparation & Cooking
Trim off stalk ends, peel thinly, then quarter or slice (according to size and recipe). Cook, covered, in boiling salted water 20 to 25 minutes, until tender; allow a few minutes longer if steaming. Kohlrabi may also be cooked, then peeled, if desired.

Serving Suggestions
Small kohlrabi can be eaten raw. It is delicious peeled and grated or chopped in salads—the crisp texture and sweet, delicate flavor (similar to that of a young turnip) add bite and interest. Or coat the grated vegetable in a lightly curried mayonnaise and spoon into crisp lettuce cups to serve as an original first course.

Add diced kohlrabi to casseroles, stock and soups or use as you would turnips and rutabagas. Try it cooked and tossed in melted butter, hollandaise or a cream sauce; or coated with béchamel, sprinkled with cheese and broiled until golden. Stuffed kohlrabi is also excellent: hollow out vegetable, fill with a tasty meat stuffing and poach in stock until tender.

Kohlrabi

Cauliflower

The cauliflower *(Brassica oleracea* var. *botrytis cauliflora)* originated in the Mediterranean region and first appeared in England and France around the end of the 16th century.

Both summer and winter varieties are available throughout the year. On summer cauliflowers the leaves are opened out around the head (known as curds), but on winter types the leaves are folded over the head. Green flowering varieties are available too.

Buying & Storing
Size does not denote quality. Choose cauliflowers with creamy white (or green), firm, compact heads. Do not buy those where the white flower heads are beginning to open. If not using immediately, store, loosely wrapped in a plastic bag, in the crisper drawer of the refrigerator up to two days.

Preparation & Cooking
To cook whole, cut off all but the smallest, tender inner leaves, wash thoroughly and make a deep cross in the bottom of the stalk. Cook, covered, in a small amount of boiling salted water 12 to 15 minutes, so that it steam-cooks (the stem in the boiling water and the head in the steam) until just tender. To cook flowerets, break or cut in even pieces and cook five to six minutes. Cauliflower, whole or flowerets, may also be steamed (sprinkled with lemon juice), if desired; allow a few minutes extra cooking time.

Serving Suggestions
Use small flowerets and small slices of crunchy stalk raw in salads or with dips. They are also good parboiled and tossed (still warm) in vinaigrette. Serve chilled with red kidney beans and flaked tuna or peeled shrimp as a first course.

Hot cauliflower is delicious drizzled with browned butter and a sprinkling of fresh herbs, or coated with a rich white or cheese sauce. Or cook it whole Polonaise-style; garnish with butter-crisp bread crumbs, parsley, sieved egg yolk and finely chopped egg white. Try cauliflowerets, braised in butter and a little stock spiced with mace, as an accompaniment. Cauliflower also makes a tasty soup.

Napa Cabbage

Napa cabbage leaves *(Brassica pekinensis)* are also known as Chinese leaves, celery cabbage or *pe-tsai*—and sometimes, incorrectly, as Chinese cabbage, see page 8. Although this is a relatively new vegetable to Western countries, it has been known in China and Asia since the 5th century.

Napa cabbage looks rather like a cross between a head of celery and a Cos lettuce—being long, slender and tightly-packed with pale-green leaves on the edges of thick, white crisp rib-stems.

Buying & Preparation
Napa cabbage is available throughout the year. It can be quite large, so are often sold in halves. Choose firm heads and store up to one week in the crisper drawer.

To prepare, trim off bottom, rinse in cold water, then pat dry. Chop, slice, shred or separate in stems.

Serving Suggestions
This deliciously crisp and juicy vegetable is good to eat both raw and cooked. It is used extensively in Chinese dishes.

The tender inner leaves are excellent shredded raw into salads and coleslaws. Serve the stems cut in sticks with cheese and crusty bread.

Try the outer leaves sliced and stir-fried in a little garlic-flavored oil until tender-crisp, or shred and add to soups.

The juicy stems make succulent eating: trim off green leafy parts and either braise stems with butter and onions, or simmer until just tender and serve tossed in melted butter or cream and herbs.

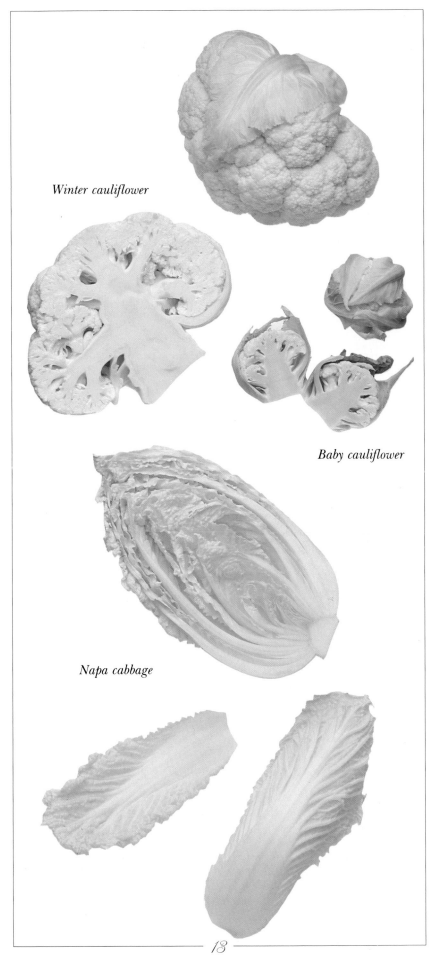

Winter cauliflower

Baby cauliflower

Napa cabbage

Broccoli

Broccoli (*Brassica oleracea* var. *italica*) is a member of the Brassica family. It originally came from Asia Minor and the Mediterranean region, and was first cultivated in Italy in the 16th century. The small purple sprouting type, with small clusters of purple flowers sprouting up the stem, is widely known in northern Europe. White and green varieties are also available. Calabrese or Italian broccoli has larger flower heads on the stems; it is imported from Italy. Broccoli and calabrese are completely interchangeable and are cooked and eaten in the same way.

Broccoli is available virtually all year-round and calabrese from midsummer through to early winter.

Buying & Storing
Choose broccoli and calabrese with tight compact heads and firm stalks which snap easily. Both types store well, wrapped loosely in plastic bags, in the crisper drawer of the refrigerator up to three days.

Preparation & Cooking
Trim off tough lower part of stems and divide thicker stalks in half to ensure even cooking. Cook them covered, in very little boiling salted water five to ten minutes (or steam 10 to 12 minutes) until tender-crisp. To prevent overcooking the more tender flower heads, tie broccoli spears together in bundles and stand upright in a small pan, so that stalks boil while the flower heads only steam.

Broccoli is good stir-fried: divide flower heads and slice stalks.

Serving Suggestions
Tender, young broccoli and calabrese spears are good cut up and eaten raw in salads—or parboiled until nutty-crisp. Cooked this way they are also excellent served with dips and fondues. Blanched spears, wrapped in puff pastry and baked, or dipped into a light batter and fried, are perfect served with a tasty dip.

Broccoli is delicious served with a sauce, such as butter with capers or toasted sliced almonds, or covered with a tangy cheese and herb sauce, sprinkled with buttered crumbs and baked. A mixture of broccoli and cauliflower flowerets, parboiled, then stir-fried in a spicy butter, see page 107, makes a good accompaniment. Pureed broccoli makes an excellent soup.

Kale

Kale (*Brassica oleracea* var. *acephala*) is native to the Eastern Mediterranean and Asia Minor. It is also known as curly kale. A cabbage without a solid head (or heart), it can be flat or curly with heavily crimped leaves and prominent midribs, and varies in color from dark-green to purple. Kale has coarse-textured leaves and a stronger flavor than other cabbages.

Buying & Storing
Kale is in season during winter and spring. Choose fresh looking plants, avoiding any that are wilted or yellowing. Kale will keep two to three days in a plastic bag in the crisper drawer of the refrigerator.

Preparation & Cooking
Cut off root end, strip leaves from stalks and tear in two or three pieces, or shred coarsely. Cover and cook in boiling salted water (or braise with a little stock and butter) about ten minutes, until tender, or steam 12 to 15 minutes. Drain thoroughly before serving.

Serving Suggestions
Kale has a rather pronounced flavor and for this reason is best served on its own as an accompaniment. Serve it tossed in melted butter and plenty of pepper, or drizzled with cream, snipped chives and crisp fried bacon. It is also good served with béchamel sauce.

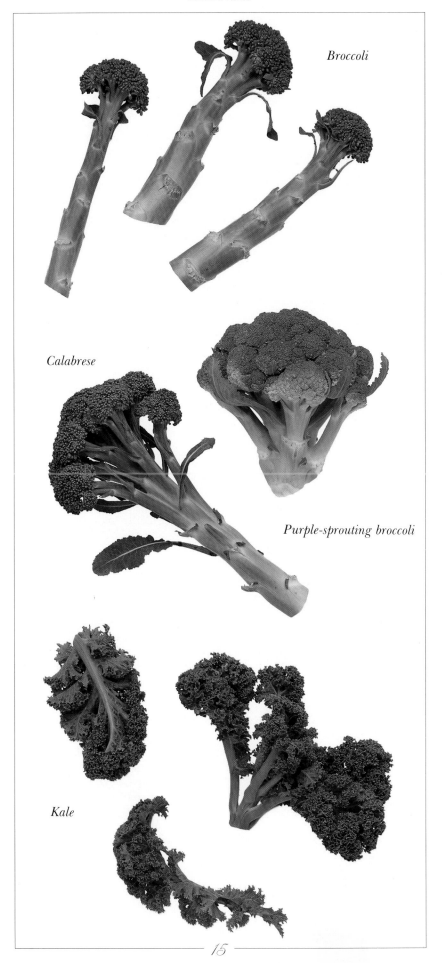

Broccoli

Calabrese

Purple-sprouting broccoli

Kale

Lettuce

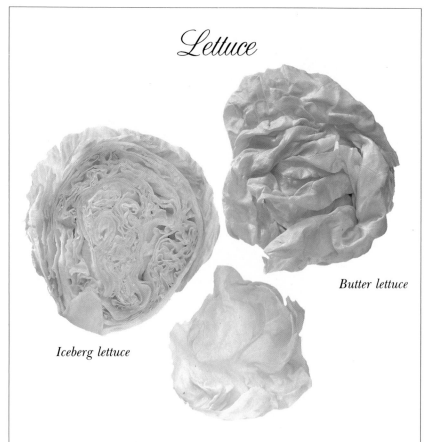

Butter lettuce

Iceberg lettuce

The lettuce (*Lactuca sativa*) that was cultivated in England in the 15th century was more likely for cooking than eating raw. Suggestions as to its origins range from the Mediterranean to Siberia!

Lettuces come in many shapes and sizes, but there are three main groups: the cabbage or butterhead type, the cos (or romaine) lettuce and the loose-leaf lettuce.

Cabbage lettuces have round heads and range from the soft round lettuce to the crisp delicious Webb's Wonderful, the crunchy, tight-hearted icebergs and the dwarf hearty Little Gem with its sweet flavor.

The cos lettuce is a crisp, flavorsome, long-leaved lettuce. A red-leaved cos is now available.

Loose-leaf lettuce varieties include the curly light-green leaved Salad Bowl, the red oak-leaf type (also called *Feuille de Chêne)* and Lollo Rosso, a frilly red-edged lettuce with a slightly bitter flavor.

Celtuce is a lesser known non-heading variety, with stiff green leaves on a stem, which is also eaten. It is often called asparagus lettuce, as its flavor is a cross between asparagus and lettuce.

Buying & Storing
Lettuces are available all year and there will generally be several varieties to choose from. Whichever you buy, it should be fresh with a good color. Lettuce is best eaten fresh, although most types will keep in the crisper drawer of the refrigerator two to five days.

Preparation
Trim bottom of lettuce and remove any tough outer leaves, then wash and dry before using. It is better to tear lettuce with your hands, as cutting it with a knife causes bruising and discoloring. If shredded lettuce is required, do it at the last moment.

Serving Suggestions
Lettuce is mainly used in salads, ranging from simple green salads to the more elaborate Caesar, Waldorf and Niçoise. It is also very tasty cooked: stir-fry shredded lettuce hearts or braise in butter and stock or wine and serve drizzled with cream and chopped herbs. Lettuce and sorrel soup is quite delicious—serve chilled, topped with dairy sour cream.

Webb's wonderful lettuce

Lollo Rosso

Oak-leaf lettuce

Litte Gem lettuce

Cos lettuce

Chicory

Chicory (*Cichorium intybus*) has been cultivated in Europe since around the end of the 13th century. It is related to endive and is known as *chicorée frisée* in France.

There are two basic types: chicory has narrow curly leaves, with dark-green outer leaves and very pale inner ones; escarole (often called Batavian endive or Batavia) is broader-leaved and less curly. Some chicory are tightly-packed and have a blue-green tinge, others are looser-leaved. Both types of chicory are bitter-flavored, although escarole is less so.

Chicory is in the shops all year-round—choose one with a nice light center as the darker the leaves, the more bitter the flavor.

Both types are best eaten freshly purchased, but can be stored briefly in a plastic bag in the crisper drawer of the refrigerator.

Serving Suggestions
Once washed, trimmed and dried, the leaves are included in salads and salad-based hors d'oeuvres, where they are excellent dressed in a good, strong vinaigrette to complement their bitter flavor. Chicory looks especially attractive used on open sandwiches and as a garnish. The leaves are also delicious lightly sautéed in butter.

Endive

Endive (*Cichorium endiva*) was developed from the wild plant succory, a native of Europe. Belgian endive, the most familiar type, is also known as white chicory, sometimes simply endive in France, and Witloof chicory in Belgium.

Belgian endive is produced by cutting off the natural foliage and forcing the roots (in the dark) to yield long, white tight-packed heads of leaves (or white chicons).

Available from autumn to spring; look for conical, crisp, white, tightly-packed heads, avoiding any with green tips—these will be bitter. Endive is best eaten fresh, but can be kept wrapped in dark paper, to preserve the white color, in the refrigerator two to three days.

Preparation & Cooking
Cut off root bottom, remove any damaged outer leaves and wash. Leave whole, divide in leaves or slice, as required. To cook whole, blanch in boiling water with lemon juice added four to five minutes, or steam six to seven minutes. Or braise in butter and stock.

Serving Suggestions
Raw endive is a delicious addition to salads; it goes particularly well with citrus fruits and nuts. Parboiled Belgian endive, wrapped in ham, coated with cheese sauce and baked *au gratin* is good. Or try it braised in butter and wine with shallots and tomatoes, or steamed and tossed in melted butter or cream and herbs.

Radicchio

Radicchio (*Cichorium intybus* var. *foliosum*), or red chicory, originated in Italy. It is closely related to endive. There are several types: forced radicchio resembles Belgian endive in shape and size, and has a white head with dark red-edged leaves; Rossa de Treviso is more open with dark-red oblong leaves and creamy-white stalks; Rossa di Veronia is round, like a small, tight lettuce head, with cerise leaves and white stalks and veins. All types are similar in flavor to chicory.

This vegetable has become increasingly popular for its attractive color, in salads and hors d'oeuvres. It is served raw or cooked in the same way as chicory, see above.

Chicory

Escarole

Chicory

Belgian endive

Radicchio (Rossa di Verona)

Radicchio (Rossa de Treviso)

Spinach

Spinach (*Spinacia oleracea*) has vague origins: some say it originated in Persia, others that it is native to the Far East. It was certainly eaten by the Greeks and Romans and arrived in northern Europe during the 16th century.

There are two types of true spinach: a summer variety and a winter spinach, making it available throughout the year. True spinach or English spinach has a more delicate flavor than other types.

New Zealand spinach (*Tetragonia expansa*) is not spinach at all, but it does come from New Zealand! It has a mild, sweet flavor with smaller, tougher leaves than true spinach.

Beet greens (*Beta vulgaris* var. *cicla*) are coarser in texture—but grow year-round, even in the coldest weather. It makes a good substitute when true spinach is unavailable. If you've a patch of soil to spare, this is a good vegetable to grow: keep picking the leaves throughout the year to ensure a constant supply of new, young, tender ones.

Buying & Storing
Spinach wilts quickly, so buy as fresh as possible and use quickly. If using for cooking, rather than salads, store in the refrigerator in a plastic bag up to two days.

Preparation & Cooking
Spinach must be washed thoroughly in several changes of cold water as the slightest speck of grit or sand will ruin the finished dish. Discard tough center stems. Shake off excess moisture and pack spinach into a large saucepan. Do not add any water—the moisture clinging to the leaves is sufficient for cooking. Cover tightly and cook gently, turning occasionally, until spinach decreases in volume. Bring to a boil and cook eight to ten minutes, until tender. Drain well in a colander and sieve, pressing spinach firmly against the side with a saucer to force out all moisture.

Serving Suggestions
When young and tender (and very fresh), spinach leaves in a good dressing make an excellent salad—on their own or with a selection of mixed salad leaves and other ingredients, see page 14.

Spinach leaves may be shredded and stirred into Chinese soups and are delicious stir-fried briefly with flavorings, such as gingerroot, garlic and chiles.

Cooked, pureed or chopped spinach forms an excellent basis for soups, soufflés and crepe fillings. Mixed with cream, eggs and cheese, it makes a delicious quiche.

To serve as an accompaniment, toss cooked spinach in melted butter, seasonings and a pinch of grated nutmeg. For a richer dish, mix with whipping cream and chopped herbs, or coat spinach with béchamel. Sprinkle with Emmenthaler cheese and broil until golden.

Sorrel

Sorrel (*Rumex acetosa*) grows wild in most European regions. Of the two main varieties available, the French type is considered better for cooking, as it has a mild flavor. Sorrel is actually a herb which is served as a vegetable, in similar ways to spinach, see above.

The succulent leaves, shaped like elongated arrowheads, are green and glossy with a slightly acid, sharp flavor. They are highly prized in France and used in a variety of dishes.

Buying & Storing
Sorrel is not widely available, although you may find that produce markets stock it during the summer. It is best eaten fresh, though it can be stored in a plastic bag in the refrigerator two to three days.

If growing your own sorrel—and it is well worth doing so, either from seed or buy a small pot from your local garden center—pick the leaves when young and small as they become very bitter if left to grow large.

Beet greens

English spinach

French sorrel

This also encourages the plant to produce more leaves.

Preparation & Cooking
Pick off and discard stems. Wash leaves well and shake dry. Cook as for spinach, see opposite page, a few minutes until tender, or sauté in a little butter over low heat until wilted and tender. Chop or puree and use as required.

Serving Suggestions
Sorrel is a wonderful addition to green salads and is also good chopped and added to omelets. A few leaves added to fish before baking impart an excellent flavor. Pureed sorrel, mixed with cream and stock, makes a favorite soup. Use the puree for soufflés, or as an unusual base for eggs Florentine, instead of spinach. Pureed sorrel is a perfect accompaniment to veal and fish dishes.

Watercress

Watercress *(Nasturtium officinale)* is an aquatic plant that grows wild in freshwater streams throughout Europe. It is also widely cultivated in watercress beds in several countries.

Buying & Storing
Watercress is available all year, sold in bunches or ready-trimmed in vacuum packs. Choose watercress with dark-green, glossy leaves. Unopened packs keep in the refrigerator up to three days; bunches should be kept in a plastic bag in the refrigerator and used within one day. To freshen watercress, place bunches' leaves down in a bowl of cold water several hours. Wash well and trim stems before using.

Serving Suggestions
Watercress makes an excellent garnish and is splended in salads—try it with sections of orange and Belgian endive, tossed in a tangy walnut oil dressing.

Mixed with shredded radicchio, it makes a colorful and unusual bed for shrimp cocktails. Use the finely chopped leaves to flavor and color butters and dips, and to prepare stuffings—especially good for lamb or fish. Add whole leaves to omelets, quiches and stir-fry dishes.

Serve a watercress sauce with fish or veal, and watercress mayonnaise with cold salmon. Watercress soup is delicious, served hot or cold.

AMERICAN CRESS & WINTER CRESS

American cress *(Barbarea praecox)*, or land cress as it is also known, is native to America. Winter cress *(Barbarea vulgaris)* from Europe is closely related. These are both similar in flavor to watercress and far easier to grow at home in a shady, damp corner of the garden. Prepare and use both as you would watercress.

Winter cress

Watercress

Lamb's lettuce

Salad cress

Salad Cress

Salad cress *(Lepidium sativum)* is sometimes incorrectly called mustard and cress. At one time cress was grown from a mixture of pepper cress seeds and mustard seeds; however, nowadays most commercially grown cress is produced from rape seeds only.

Salad cress is available all year-round and is sold in small bunches, still growing. These bunches keep fresh up to three days stored in a plastic bag in the crisper drawer of the refrigerator.

To use, snip off cress, wash thoroughly and pat dry. Use in salads and sandwich fillings; it is especially good with egg and cream cheese mixture, or as a garnish. Salad cress also makes a crisp and interesting omelet or savory crepe fillings, mixed with crisp fried bacon and grated cheese.

Lamb's Lettuce

Lamb's lettuce *(Valerianella locusto)*, also known as corn salad and as *mâche* in France, has been cultivated from the wild variety which grows in cornfields. The plant has small, soft, green leaves (the shape of lamb's tongues) with a velvety texture and a delicate flavor.

Look for lamb's lettuce in produce markets and supermarkets throughout the year. It is a hardy plant to grow at home and makes a good winter substitute for lettuce.

Wash, pat dry and use with other leaves in salads or as a decorative border for mousses and pâtés. It is also good lightly sautéed in butter as an accompaniment.

Dandelion

The dandelion *(Taraxacum officinale)* is believed to be one of the bitter herbs mentioned in the Old Testament. Although generally regarded as a most persistent weed, various strains of dandelion plant are cultivated. The cultivated types are larger than the wild dandelion, tightly-packed with dark-green leaves and white stems.

Cultivated dandelions are sometimes available from produce markets during the summer. The wild type should be picked in early spring while young and tender; do not pick from roadsides where they may have been chemically sprayed. Wash thoroughly before use.

Serving Suggestions

The leaves have a slightly bitter flavor which is good in salads; sprinkle the flower petals on top for a pretty effect. Or use them in the classic French salad *Salade de Pissenlits au Lard,* a combination of dandelion leaves, crisp fried bacon and croutons, dressed in a vinaigrette with the hot bacon fat poured over the salad before serving. Add shredded leaves to stir-fry dishes.

The roots are used, dried and ground, to make a coffee substitute which is sold in health-food stores.

Nettle

The stinging nettle *(Urtica dioica)* is one of the most common edible wild plants, growing abundantly in almost any environment. At one time nettle beds were a feature in gardens—the nettles being prized for their nutritional quality.

Nettles are around in spring and summer. Incidentally, once cooked the sting is destroyed!

Nettles are extremely good when young. The best time to pick them is when the tender shoots are still short, or remove the tops and pale-green leaves of more mature plants (the darker leaves are coarse and unpleasantly bitter). Avoid those near roadsides which may have been sprayed with chemicals.

Preparation & Cooking

Remove stems from nettles and wash thoroughly, still wearing rubber gloves. Shake off excess moisture and cook in a tightly covered pan, with only the moisture clinging to the leaves after washing, 10 to 15 minutes, until tender. Drain well, then chop or puree and serve.

Serving Suggestions

Toss in melted butter and seasonings and serve as an accompaniment, or as a base for Florentine-style poached eggs. Serve with a béchamel sauce or parboil and sauté in butter with green onions and garlic; stir in a small amount of cream just before serving. Nettles also make a delicious soup, see page 75.

Rocket

Rocket *(Eruca sativa)* is native to the Mediterranean region and grows wild in many parts of Europe. Related to the cresses, rocket has pinnately lobed leaves with a slightly hot, peppery flavor. The cultivated varieties are more tender and milder than the wild type.

Rocket may be found in Greek and Italian ethnic markets, and some-times in supermarkets. It grows easily from seed and is worth planting in your garden to experiment with and enjoy its unusual flavor.

Sparingly snipped into salads, rocket is especially good, or try it combined with green onions and tomatoes in a tangy dressing as an unusual first course. Sprinkle over soups as a flavorful garnish.

Rocket

Nettle

Dandelion

Potato

Maris bard

Maris piper

The potato *(Solanum tuberosum)* must be the most popular vegetable worldwide—yet it came to Europe as recently as the 16th century.

There are two potato crops: thin-skinned or new potatoes and thick-skinned or mature potatoes. Selecting the right type for a recipe is important: the new or waxy types are good for salads, sautéing and boiling. The mature or thick-skinned types are better for baking, roasting and pureeing. There are many varieties from which to choose.

Buying & Storing

New potatoes arrive in the stores in late spring and remain available until the end of the summer, although imported new potatoes are available at other times during the year. Test for freshness by make sure the skins rub off easily. Buy in quantities you need and use within 48 hours.

Mature potatoes are around from late summer to late spring. In autumn their pulp is still a little waxy but becomes less so during storage. Potatoes keep well stored in a cool, frost-free place, in the large brown sacks or bags in which they come from the supplier. If purchased in plastic bags, remove and store in a cool, dry, dark, airy place.

Preparation & Cooking

Boil or steam new potatoes in their skins, or very thinly scraped, in salted water 15 minutes, or until just tender. A sprig of mint added to the water helps bring out the flavor. If you prefer not to eat new potatoes in their skins, peel after cooking.

Mature potatoes may also be cooked in their skins, or peeled very thinly. Cut in uniform sizes, cover and cook gently in boiling salted water (or steam—they are less likely to go mushy) 20 minutes, or until tender. Drain, return to pan and shake briefly over low heat to dry before using.

Serving Suggestions

Crisp, golden sautéed potatoes, cooked with onion and bacon, are delicious; so too are baked potatoes served with butter, or dairy sour cream and chives.

Mashed with butter and cream and a pinch of nutmeg, potatoes make a good accompaniment for rich dishes. Serve them mashed and piped in nests, Duchesse-style. Gratin Dauphinoise (potatoes layered and baked with garlic and cream) makes an ideal dinner accompaniment, as do Pommes Dauphine—pureed potatoes blended with choux paste, then piped and deep-fried to light, golden puffs.

Romano

King Edward

Pentland

Charlotte

Belle de Fontenay

Yam

The yam (*Dioscorea alata*) is a tropical tuber often mistaken for the sweet potato. Perhaps the confusion arises because sweet potatoes are known as yams in the southern states of America. Originally yams came from Africa, but many varieties are now grown in tropical countries. They can grow to enormous sizes, weighing as much as 50 pounds, but those available in western countries, usually weigh about one pound. The large ones are often cut in smaller pieces to sell.

Yams are available all year-round from West Indian and African ethnic markets and produce markets. The bark-like skin is tough and thick and varies from light- to dark-brown in color. The flesh may be white, yellow or sometimes pink. Whole yams store well for several weeks in a cool, dry, dark place; if in pieces, cover with plastic wrap and use within a week.

Preparation & Cooking
Cut off thick woody skin and, if not cooking immediately, drop into a bowl of cold water with lemon juice added to prevent discoloration. Dice, slice or cut in pieces, then cook in boiling salted water 20 to 30 minutes, until tender. Drain, return to pan and shake over low heat a few minutes to dry off.

Serving Suggestions
Serve tossed in butter flavored with cinnamon, nutmeg and brown sugar or puree with butter, seasonings and herbs.

Yams may also be baked and served like baked potatoes, parboiled, sliced and sautéed or frittered. Or added to spicy soups, casseroles and curries.

Yucca Root

Yucca root (*Manihot esculenta*), also known as cassava and sweet manioc, is native to the West Indies, Africa and South America. It is a strange looking starchy tuber which is long, hairy and cylindrical, tapering at one end. It is from this vegetable that we get tapioca.

Yucca root is available in Asian ethnic markets. It keeps well in a cool, airy place several weeks.

Preparation & Cooking
Peel off the hairy, bark-like skin, cut in even pieces and cook, covered, in boiling salted water 20 minutes, or until tender.

Serving Suggestions
Serve and eat yucca root as you would potatoes. As the flavor is rather bland, pep it up with herbs and seasonings—perhaps a dash of lemon or lime juice.

Yucca root is good mashed, or parboiled and then sautéed. The pulp may also be cut in chips, coated in batter, deep-fried and served with a tasty dip.

Sweet Potato

The sweet potato (*Ipomoea batatas*) was common in Europe during the 16th and 17th centuries and, in fact, came before the ordinary potato. It then gradually faded as the ordinary potato became a favorite. The two are not related.

You will find sweet potatoes in supermarkets, produce markets and West Indian ethnic markets during winter and spring. The skin color varies according to variety; the smooth, red-skinned type is the one usually available. Buy smooth, firm tubers and store in a cool, dry, airy place (not the refrigerator) up to three days.

Preparation & Cooking
Scrub, peel and slice or cut even pieces and simmer gently in salted water 15 to 20 minutes until tender. The pulp is soft and floury when cooked; it will break up if boiled rapidly. Sweet potatoes may also be

Yucca root

Red sweet potatoes

Yams

boiled in their skins and peeled after cooking.

Serving Suggestions
Serve sweet potatoes as you would ordinary potatoes, either boiled, mashed with butter and seasonings, or deep-fried. Their delicous sweet flavor makes them a natural for serving glazed or candied. Bake in a mixture of brown sugar, spices, butter and orange juice; cooked this way, they make a perfect accompaniment for turkey or chicken. Try them baked or roasted around a roast, too. Thin slivers of sweet potato, dipped into batter and fried, are also good, see page 89.

Jerusalem Artichoke

The Jerusalem artichoke (*Helianthus tuberosus*) or sunchoke is a native of North Africa and has no historical connection with Jerusalem. The word is believed to be a misinterpretation of *girasole*, the Italian name for sunflower, to which the Jerusalem artichoke is related.

There are two types, red and white. The white, actually light-brown in color, has a finer flavor and is more widely available. In season throughout the winter, Jerusalem artichokes look rather like knobbly new potatoes. Buy those that feel firm, as they soften and wrinkle with age. They will keep successfully up to three days in a cool, dry, dark place.

Preparation & Cooking

Peeling Jerusalem artichokes is a tiresome job, so cook the scrubbed tubers in their skins and peel them afterwards—it's quicker and easier.

Cook whole artichokes in lightly salted boiling water about ten minutes if unpeeled, six to seven minutes if peeled. Cook sliced or diced ones five minutes. Artichokes may also be steamed, or cooked in their skins in a hot oven 30 to 40 minutes. Pierce with a skewer to test—they should be just tender when ready.

Serving Suggestions

Boiled or steamed artichokes are delicious left whole, tossed in lemon and parsley butter and sprinkled with crisp, crumbled bacon. Coat with a rich cheese or tomato sauce. Pureed they make excellent soup, enriched with butter and cream or an egg yolk. They are very good sliced and sautéed in garlic butter or cooked Dauphinoise style, see page 104. Jerusalem artichokes may also be served raw in salads; peel and grate them into a lemon or vinegar dressing (to prevent discoloration) before mixing with other ingredients.

Chinese Artichoke

The Chinese artichoke (*Stachys affinis*), a native of the Far East, is especially prized in France. Chinese artichokes are smaller than Jerusalem artichokes, creamy-colored, with tapering ends. They have a delicate flavor and are best served simply.

Preparation & Cooking

Wash and cook in their skins (they do not need peeling) in boiling salted water, or a little chicken stock, 10 to 12 minutes, until tender but still crisp. Drain and toss in melted butter. Serve warm with a delicate vinaigrette.

Jicama

Jicama (*Pachyrrhizus erosus*) is native to Mexico and looks rather like a turnip with a thin brown skin. It is sometimes called yam bean. Jicama varies in size from one to six pounds and is often sold cut in smaller pieces. The white pulp resembles that of the water chestnut in taste and texture.

Buying & Storing

Choose small to medium-size jicama, as these have a better texture than the larger ones, which can be woody. The whole vegetable keeps well in a cool, dry, dark place up to two weeks. Cover cut pieces with plastic wrap and refrigerate up to one week.

Preparation & Cooking

Scrub well in cold water, peel, then slice thinly, shred, dice or cut in julienne strips. Cook in boilng salted water about 20 minutes, or steam until tender. Serve raw in salads or as an appetizer with dips. Try it stir-fried, too.

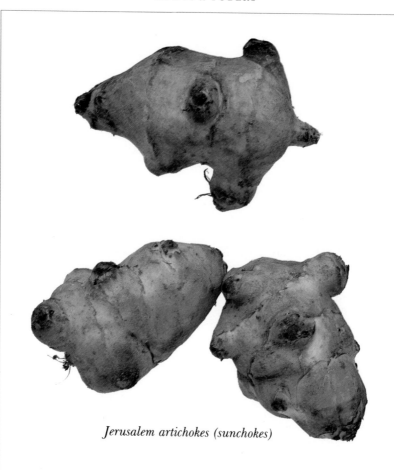

Jerusalem artichokes (sunchokes)

Chinese artichoke

Salsify

Salsify (*Tragopogon porrifolius*) belongs to the daisy family and is a native of southern Europe. It is a long, white pulp root with a tender, pale skin. It is sometimes referred to as the oyster plant because its flavor is similar to that of oysters. The flavor is delicate and worth trying.

Buying & Storing
Salsify is in the stores from autumn through to late spring. Look for young ones with fresh greyish-green leaves and tapering roots; avoid those that are limp wtih dry, shrivelled skins. Salsify will keep two to three days, stored in the crisper drawer of the refrigerator.

Preparation & Cooking
The leaves of salsify are edible and very good shredded raw into salads; they may also be cooked in the same way as spinach, see page 20. Scrub salsify in cold water, cut off top and taping root end and scrape off skin.

Cut in even pieces. If not cooking immediately, place in cold water with a spoonful of lemon juice or vinegar added to keep the pulp white. Cook in boiling salted water 20 to 30 minutes or until tender.

Serving Suggestions
Salsify is delicious served wth béarnaise or mornay sauce, or tossed in melted butter flavored with anchovies. Cream of salsify soup is excellent: cook the vegetable with onions and stock until very tender, then puree and reheat with cream, seasonings and chopped herbs. Salsify fritters are extremely tasty. Parboil the vegetable in fingers or slices, then dip into a light batter. Deep-fry until golden and serve with tartar or spiced tomato sauce.

To prepare a salad, cut salsify in small pieces and cook as above; drain and toss while still warm in a vinaigrette. Chill before mixing with sliced green onions, herbs and corn salad.

Scorzonera

Scorzonera (*Scorzonera hispanica*), or black salsify as it is known, simply looks like a black-skinned version of salsify. Although the dark skin may look unappetizing, the pulp inside is white and tastes very similar to

salsify—in fact, many people claim it has a better, more pronounced flavor.

Scorzonera is available during the winter until late spring. Prepare and cook as salsify, see above.

Taro Root

The taro root (*Colocasia esculenta* var. *antiquorum*) is a starchy vegetable, used as a staple food in the West Indies, India and West Africa. It is called eddoe in England, *dasheen* in Indian and West Indian ethnic markets and *kolocassi* in Greek stores.

Available in summer, taro root comes in many sizes and has a rough brown exterior. Select those which feel firm; they will keep in the crisper drawer of the refrigerator four to five days.

The leaves of the taro root are called taro or dasheen leaves. They are large, thick and fleshy and are also

available during the summer.

Preparation & Cooking
Wash, peel and slice taro root, or cut in even pieces, and cook and serve as you would potatoes, see page 26. It may be boiled and mashed, sliced and fried, or added to casseroles and curries. Try it boiled and tossed in garlic butter with plenty of seasoning, or spiced with a few drops of hot-pepper sauce.

Taro leaves have a slightly bitter flavor and are prepared in the same way as kale, see page 14.

Taro root (eddoe)

Scorzonera

Radish

The radish (*Raphanus sativus*) is an ancient vegetable believed to have originated in southern Asia, although some experts say its place of origin was Egypt.

There are many different types of radish, all varying in flavor, shape and color. Some are hot and pungent; some are small, round and scarlet. Others are elongated and pale in color, often with white tips.

Radishes are usually quite small, although the white radish can be six to seven inches long. During the winter, Spanish or black radishes are sometimes available: these have a large bulbous root with white pulp and are stronger and coarser than the smaller types.

Buying & Preparation

Available more or less all year. Look for smooth, bright-looking radishes. The leaves wilt quickly and are not a good indication of quality. To check for freshness, it is best to squeeze radishes gently—they should feel firm, never spongy or soft. Wash and store in plastic bags in the crisper drawer of the refrigerator four to five days.

To prepare, trim off root ends and tops and drop into iced water an hour or so before cooking.

Serving Suggestions

The French enjoy radishes spread with butter, dipped into salt and eaten with crusty French bread. The smaller red radishes are a nice addition to salads—either whole, quartered or sliced. White and black radishes should be grated before adding to salads.

Radishes make pretty roses for garnishing. To make a radish rose, trim away root ends and larger leaves, leaving on the smallest leaf. Using a small, sharp, pointed knife, cut three petals from root end to leaf end of radish, taking care not to cut right through. Place radish roses in iced water until opened.

Radishes are also good served hot. Try them sautéed or stir-fried, steamed or braised and served with a butter or cream sauce.

Daikon

The daikon (*Raphanus sativus* var. *longipinnatus*), also known as mooli, is a popular vegetable in some parts of Asia and has been grown for many centuries in China and Japan.

The daikon is closely related to the radish but it actually looks like a giant white carrot. It has a crisp, crunchy texture and a milder flavor than the more familiar red radish. Daikon is available throughout the year.

When buying daikon, buy the clean, fresh ones which feel hard—limp daikons may well be spongy and dry inside. Trim root end and top, then peel thinly to prepare.

Daikon will keep well up to a week stored in a cool, dry place or in a plastic bag in the crisper drawer of the refrigerator.

Serving Suggestions

Slice or grate for adding raw to salads, or use grated as a sandwich filling. Cut in fingers; raw daikon makes an excellent crudité. Grate or shred a daikon into clear, broth-style soups to add bite and flavor.

Try serving daikon as a hot accompaniment. Slice and cook in lightly salted boiling water three to four minutes, then drain and toss in butter or cream and freshly ground pepper. Thinly sliced, it can be stir-fried with other ingredients. Daikon is also good braised in butter and stock.

The Japanese use this vegetable frequently, often finely grated and added to dips and sauces, and carved in shapes as a garnish.

Daikon

Radishes

Beet

Beet (*Beta vulgaris*) is thought to have been cultivated in the Middle East about 2000 years ago. The Greeks and Romans grew the vegetable for its leaves. Although today we enjoy beets for its roots, the leaves are, in fact, tasty and nutritious, similar in flavor to spinach and may be cooked in the same way, see page 20.

Buying & Storing
Beets are available all year; the baby variety, available at their peak during summer, are especially sweet and delicious. Look for raw beets with smooth skins and hard roots.

Canned beets are also available; buy them unpeeled whenever possible. Beets are also sold in vacuum packs, cooked and peeled and often flavored with vinegar; check for suitability if using them in a specific recipe.

Raw beets keep week in a cool place up to one week. Cooked they will keep in the refrigerator up to three days.

Preparation & Cooking
Twist off leafy tops, leaving about 1 inch of stems; do not trim root ends unless a recipe states otherwise. Rinse, taking care not to break the skins or beets will bleed and lose color during cooking. Cook in boiling salted water 45 minutes to 1-1/2 hours, according to size. To test if cooked, lift from pan and press gently; if peel slips off easily, it is cooked. Or bake beets in foil in the oven as you would potatoes. Peel while warm and use as required.

Serving Suggestions
Good in hot dishes and accompaniments as well as salads, relishes and pickles. Try it grated or diced and served warm in a herbed vinaigrette, or cold in a dairy sour cream or yogurt dressing flavored with horseradish or dill. Serve hot baby beets in a creamy béchamel or cheese sauce as an accompaniment. Beets are also used to make the classic Russian soup Borscht.

Celery Root

Celery root (*Apium graveolens*) was a popular vegetable in the 18th and 19th centuries. It became less fashionable, but is now enjoying a revival. Often called celeriac, celery root is native to southern Europe.

In spite of its knobby, swollen shape, celery root is closely related to celery and has an authentic celery taste; it is similar in texture to the heart of celery. It is available during most of the winter. Select hard roots that weigh heavy in the hand. It keeps well in the crisper drawer of the refrigerator several days.

Preparation & Cooking
Peel and slice celery root and drop into a bowl of cold water with lemon juice or vinegar to prevent discoloration. Cook in boiling salted water 20 to 30 minutes, according to size, until tender, or steam, a little longer.

Serving Suggestions
Raw and coarsely grated or chopped celery root is a delicious addition to many salads. For a starter, blanch julienne strips in acidulated water two minutes. Toss while still warm in a mustard-flavored vinaigrette and serve chilled.

Cooked celery root is marvelous for flavoring soups, stocks, casseroles and sauces, and is a splendid vegetable in its own right. Serve it hot with a hollandaise, herb or butter sauce, or parboiled and baked *au gratin* with a rich cheese sauce.

Pureed celery root, flavored with nutmeg, cream and herbs, makes an excellent soup. Or mix the puree with equal amounts of mashed potato, blend with butter and seasonings, and serve sprinkled with toasted almonds. Celery root is also delicious French-fried style, see page 106.

Celery root (celeriac)

Beets

Young early turnips

Mature purple-tinged turnip

Mature green-tinged turnips

Turnip

The turnip *(Brassica campestris* var. *rapa)*, a prehistoric vegetable, was a staple food in northern Europe until potatoes gained in popularity. Too often this delicious vegetable is ignored or relegated to the stewpot—it deserves more recognition.

There are two types—early and mature. The early type has tender pulp with a more delicate flavor than the mature turnips. They usually appear in the stores in spring through to summer. Mature turnips follow on from summer through to spring. They may be round, flattened or cylindrical, yellow or white, often with a flash of green or purple near the top. Choose firm, young turnips that feel heavy for their size. They store well in a cool, dry place or refrigerator one to two weeks.

Preparation & Cooking

Trim top and root, then peel. Cook young turnips whole, quartered or sliced, either by steaming or boiling in salted water until tender. The timing varies with the age of the vegetable, but as a general guide, steam young whole turnips 20 to 30 minutes; boil older types 20 minutes if sliced, or 30 to 40 minutes if whole.

Serving Suggestions

Enjoy turnips boiled, braised, added to casseroles, pot roasts and pies—and even raw. The light and delicate, slightly peppery flavor goes well with butter and rich creamy sauces.

For a colorful combination, try thin julienne strips of carrot and turnip poached in stock and served tossed in whipping cream and chives. Pureed turnip mixed with mashed potato, butter and seasoning makes a lovely topping for fish and an unusual accompaniment for smoked sausages or meat and poultry dishes.

Whole baby turnips, parboiled, hollowed out and filled with a tasty mixture before baking, are quite delicious, see page 91.

Coarsely grate or sliver young raw turnips and add to salads. They are especially good with watercress and orange. Or try them dressed with a tangy vinaigrette or mixed into a mayonnaise potato salad.

Rutabaga

Rutabaga *(Brassica campestris* var. *rutabaga)*, Swede or Swedish turnip is sometimes confused with turnip, although it is larger and sweeter with orangy-yellow pulp. Rutabagas are believed to have originated in Bohemia in the 17th century.

These purple-orange skinned roots are in season during winter and spring. Choose medium-size rutabagas; large ones can sometimes be woody or pithy. They store well in a cool dry place several weeks.

Preparation & Cooking

Cut in quarters for easy handling, then peel and slice or dice evenly. Cooking time varies according to age but, as a guide, cook in boiling salted water 15 to 20 minutes or until tender; steaming takes a little longer. Drain well, return to pan and shake over low heat to evaporate any liquid remaining.

Serving Suggestions

Bashed neeps, the traditional accompaniment to haggis, is probably one of the most famous ways of serving rutabagas. This dish of cooked, well-mashed rutabagas, seasoned with salt, nutmeg and plenty of pepper, with butter or cream added before serving, is delicious. Slivers of raw rutabaga are an essential item in a traditional Cornish pastry.

Try rutabagas sliced and parboiled, then finished in a butter and honey glaze, or diced and braised in butter and stock, flavored with chopped parsley. Thin julienne strips, parboiled and added to stir-fry dishes, make a pleasant change.

Rutabagas

Carrot

The carrot (*Daucus carota*) originated in Afghanistan and first arrived in England from Holland. Carrots are in season all year, with baby new carrots—young early carrots—around in early summer. These are usually sold in bunches with the foliage attached. Choose firm bunches with fresh greenery. Mature carrots are larger and sold trimmed. Carrots store well in pastic bags in the crisper drawer of the refrigerator up to two weeks.

Preparation & Cooking

There is no need to peel baby carrots—simply scrub, trim and cook whole in boiling salted water or steam 10 to 15 minutes, until tender. Cooked this way they are delicious served tossed in butter with a sprinkling of fresh herbs.

Mature carrots have a stronger, richer flavor. Peel very thinly, then quarter, slice or cut in julienne strips and boil or steam until tender. Carrots are also delicious parboiled and finished by sautéing and glazing in butter.

Serving Suggestions

Carrots can be served in a variety of ways: as accompaniments; pureed in soups and soufflés; braised; added to casseroles and pot roasts; or served raw.

Baby carrots are delicious raw for dipping, or grated into a tangy dressing as a starter or side salad. For a refreshingly simple salad, cut carrots in thin strips, mix with orange-flavored mayonnaise or walnut oil dressing and arrange on a bed of mixed salad leaves. A little raw grated carrot mixed into rice just before serving adds interest and texture.

Raw mature carrots add texture and flavor to various cakes and puddings. As interesting accompaniments, serve carrots hot in a cream sauce flavored with cinnamon; mashed with pureed parsnips, enriched with butter and cream; glazed in sugar or honey; or stir-fried.

Parsnip

The parsnip (*Pastinaca sativa*) is thought to be native to the Eastern Mediterranean. Its distinctive sweet flavor is an acquired taste, it seems to be the vegetable you either love or loathe.

Parsnips are available from autumn until late spring—their flavor is said to be improved if they have been touched by frost. Choose small to medium sizes rather than large ones which may have woody center cores. They should have a crisp, clean look. Parsnips keep up to five days in the refrigerator, or three to four days in a cool dry place.

Preparation & Cooking

Scrub and trim, then peel or scrape thinly. Small ones may be left whole; otherwise halve, quarter or slice, discarding cores from larger parsnips. Cook in boiling salted water, or steam 15 to 20 minutes, depending on size, until tender. Drain well, return to pan and place over low heat a few minutes to dry.

Serving Suggestions

One of the nicest and most popular ways to cook parsnips is to parboil them, then bake around a roast. Young parsnips are good steamed and served with a creamy herbed sauce, or parboiled, dipped into batter and fried—or even deep-fried and sprinkled with parsley.

Parsnips, mashed to a smooth puree with butter, cream and a little sherry and sprinkled with toasted pine nuts, create a splended dinner party accompaniment. Another delicious idea is to cut parsnips in thin strips, wrap in well-buttered foil with plenty of seasoning and bake in a moderate oven 45 minutes, or until tender.

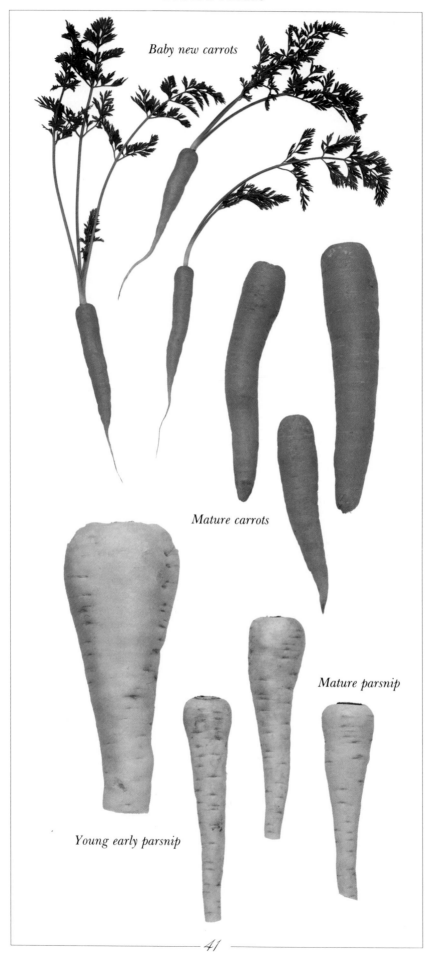

Baby new carrots

Mature carrots

Mature parsnip

Young early parsnip

Onion

The onion (*Allium cepa*) has been around for at least 5,000 years and is thought to have originated in Central Asia. The genus *Allium* includes onions of all sizes: dried, Spanish, Breton, red, pickling onions, green onions, shallots and also garlic.

Dry onions: These are the most commonly available and are in the shops all year. They are strongly flavored and come in a range of sizes, according to type. The pungent white pulp is encased in layers of papery brown or beige/white skin. Popular sweet onions include Bermuda, Maui, Vidalia and Walla Walla onions.

Spanish onions: These are large and round (larger than dry onions) and have a milder, sweeter flavor—they are delicious eaten raw. Available all year.

Red onions: These are easily recognized by their red skins and red-tinged pulp, which is mild and sweet. They vary in size. Look for red onions in produce markets and Greek and Italian ethnic markets.

Pickling onions: Also called pearl onions, these are small dry onions which are picked while the bulbs are immature. They have a strong, pungent flavor. Although generally used for pickling, they enhance many cooked dishes and may be substituted for shallots in recipes, although the flavor will be less delicate. Pickling onions are in the stores during autumn and early winter.

Green onions: These are onion sets of seed onions, harvested when young and green before the bulb has had time to form properly. Tender and mild with small white bulbs and green leaves, they are essentially a salad vegetable. They are called green shallots or scallions in Australia.

Shallots: These grow in tightly packed clusters of small bulbs. They are similar in size to pickling onions but slightly elongated in shape with a finer, more delicate flavor. They are much favored by the French in their cooking. Shallots are usually available in summer. In Australia these onions are called brown shallots.

Buying & Storing

Choose firm onions, with dry skins and store in a cool, dry place. Spanish, red and pickling onions and shallots will keep several weeks or even months if strung and hung up. Choose green onions with a crisp, fresh appearance and store in the refrigerator two to three days.

Preparation & Cooking

Trim onions and remove skins, then slice or chop as required. Blanch onions in boiling water two to three minutes at this stage to reduce their pungency, if desired. Blanching also makes them less indigestible. Drain well and pat dry before using.

Trim pickling onions and, if desired, cover with boiling water five minutes. Drain and remove skins, which will slip off.

Trim root end and leafy tops of green onions and remove any damaged outer layers.

Trim shallots, then peel before using as required.

Onions are a versatile vegetable and are delicius roasted, glazed, boiled, sautéed, stir-fried, pickled or used in chutneys.

Serving Suggestions

Use the mild, sweet-flavored onions raw in salads, or enjoy them sliced and served on crusty buttered bread, sprinkled with coarse salt.

Try shallots glazed in butter, white wine and herbs; add pickling onions whole to dishes such as Coq au Vin, or serve them sautéed in butter, or braised with tomatoes as a tasty accompaniment to pork and beef dishes.

Mild Spanish onions, thinly sliced and cooked in a creamy Madeira sauce, make an excellent vegetable course. French Onion Soup is always popular; for a change, make a smooth cream soup or a thick chowder.

Spanish onion

Dry onions

Shallots

Red onions

Green onions

Pickling onions

French Onion Tart and Pissalad-ière—two classic onion dishes—make the perfect hors d'oeuvre, lunch or supper dish. As well as being good in salads, as crudités, or as a pretty garnish, mild and tender green onions are also excellent thinly sliced and added to stir-fry dishes.

To make green onion flowers, trim onions and feather the leafy ends. Drop into a bowl of iced water and leave to curl and open. These are a popular garnish.

White-skinned garlic

Purple-skinned garlic

Garlic

Garlic *(Allium sativum)*, a close relative of the onion, is believed to be native to Central Asia and is one of the oldest of the edible *alliums*. Today garlic is grown throughout the world.

Garlic cloves (or bulbs) grow in clusters known as heads. Garlic is available all year and, according to type, the cloves may be white or purple-skinned.

Buying & Storing
Select heads of garlic which feel fat and firm, checking to see that the cloves have not dried out. Garlic stores well in a dry, airy place several weeks.

Preparation & Cooking
Break off the needed number of cloves, peel, and then slice, chop or crush as required. To crush, place cloves on a board, sprinkle with salt and, using the flat side of a knife, mash to form a smooth paste, or use a garlic press.

Although garlic may be served as a vegetable, it is more often used as a flavoring. Garlic may be used either raw or cooked; when raw it has a strong, intense flavor. Once cooked, the flavor becomes less pungent; after long, slow cooking, garlic becomes surprisingly mellow and sweet.

Serving Suggestions
Peel the cloves from one or two heads of garlic and bake them around a chicken or roast; the result will be deliciously sweet and succulent. Use one or two heads of peeled garlic cloves to great effect in garlic soups, and in rich fish soups and stews to impart a marvelous sweetness and flavor. Whole peeled cloves of garlic, simmered gently in milk until tender and then strained, make a good accompaniment to grilled steaks and chops.

The list of ideas for using garlic as a flavoring is almost endless. Rub a cut clove around a salad bowl before filling to give a delicate flavor, or steep a cut garlic clove in the salad dressing an hour or so before serving.

Rub steaks, chops and chicken portions with a cut garlic clove (or a little crushed garlic for a strong flavor) before grilling, barbecuing or frying. Cut the skin of lamb roasts and insert thin slivers of garlic before roasting. Add a crushed clove of garlic to casseroles, soups and stews to enhance the flavor of other ingredients.

Use garlic to flavor dips, pâtés, marinades and sauces, such as pesto to serve with pasta, or dressings, such as aïoli, or butter to make garlic bread and include chopped herbs for a change.

Leek

The leek *(Allium porrum)* has been around for thousands of years and was reputed to be one of the earliest cultivated vegetables. Leeks were popular in Egypt at the time of the Pharoahs, and with the Romans.

Main supplies are available from autumn through to early spring, though they are considered to be their best during the winter.

Buying & Storing

Choose straight leeks with equal proportions of green top and white stalk. Small and medium leeks are more tender than large ones. Store, unwrapped, in a cool, dark, airy place up to three days.

Preparation & Cooking

Trim off root end and a little of the green top and remove tough outer leaves. Wash thoroughly; if in any doubt as to whether they are completely clean, slit the leek down one side and hold, root end upwards, under cold running water, letting the water run through the layers. Drain upside down. Leave whole, halve, slice or finely shred.

The best ways of cooking this delicious vegetable are braising in butter with a little stock or water, or steaming. Take care not to overcook, as they easily become mushy and lose shape. Braise or simmer whole young leeks eight to ten minutes; steam 15 minutes, allowing a little longer for thicker ones.

Serving Suggestions

Leeks are excellent served hot or cold, raw or cooked. When young and tender, try them raw in salads—either shredded finely or very thinly sliced and separated in rings. Or steam, then chill and serve in a herbed vinaigrette. Cooked *à la grecque*, they are delicious served hot or chilled. Or parboil, coat with a cheese sauce and bake until golden. Chopped leeks in a cheese sauce make a good filling for pancakes. Try sliced leeks baked with eggs, cream and ham in a quiche or pie. Leeks are particularly good in soups, notably the classic Vichyssoise.

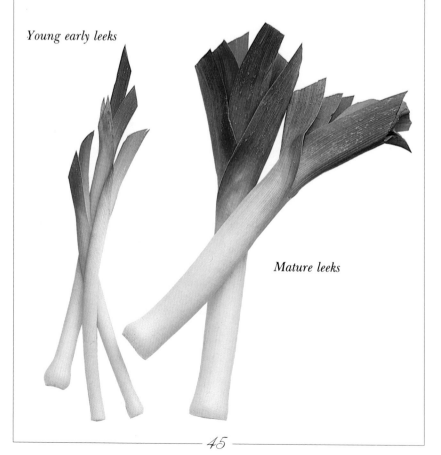

Young early leeks

Mature leeks

Green Pea

The pea *(Pisum sativum* var. *hortense)* was one of the earliest vegetables grown by man and for centuries field peas were dried to provide a staple food during winter months. Not until the 16th century did garden peas (developed in Italy) reach northern Europe.

There are two basic types of shelling pea: the ordinary garden pea and the larger "blue" pea, used for drying. Green-podded garden peas are picked when three to four inches long. The smallest, sweetest, and by far the most aristocratic of the shelling peas, is the *petit pois* which is picked when very young and tender. Peas are available fresh from spring through to late summer.

Buying & Storing
Choose firm, bright, crisp green pods which are well-filled; avoid any large ones with peas showing through. They are best eaten fresh, although they can be stored in their pods in the crisper drawer of the refrigerator two days.

Preparation & Cooking
Remove peas from pods and cook in boiling salted water five to ten minutes, according to size, until tender, or steam 10 to 15 minutes. Add a sprig of mint to flavor, if desired. Drain and, if using cold, plunge into cold water, then drain again—this retains the bright color.

Serving Suggestions
When very young and sweet, raw peas can be added to salads.

Cooked peas, tossed in butter or cream and sprinkled with mint, make a simple but excellent accompaniment. Or try *Petits Pois à la Française*—braised, buttered peas, with shallots and shredded lettuce.

Serve a puree of cooked peas, flavored with cream or bacon fat and topped with fried croutons, as an accompaniment, or use to fill pastries, pancakes or omelets.

Fresh pea soup is quite delicious, served hot or cold. Try cold, cooked peas in mayonnaise served in hollowed-out tomatoes, or use cooked peas in quiches and tartlets.

Snow Pea

Snow Pea *(Pisum sativum* var. *sacharatum)* is an edible-podded pea cultivated for its tender, succulent pod. It has a flat pod about three to four inches long and about one inch wide. The peas inside are very small.

Snow peas are now available more or less throughout the year, but are often rather expensive. The pods should look fresh green and feel crisp. They are at their best eaten fresh, but will keep in a plastic bag in the refrigerator 24 hours.

Preparation & Cooking
These peas are delicate so should be handled with care. Trim very young pods; more mature pods require stringing. Leave whole or slice, according to recipe.

Stir-frying is probably the best way to cook them, or they can be steamed five to ten minutes with butter, until just tender. Snow peas may also be cooked in boiling salted water two minutes; drain thoroughly before serving.

Serving Suggestions
Very young and tender snow peas can be served raw, whole or sliced, in salads. They are popular in Chinese stir-fried dishes. For a simple accompaniment, add them to hot oil flavored with garlic or gingerroot, and stir-fry two to three minutes.

Steamed or boiled snow peas are delicious served with a hollandaise sauce or tossed in melted butter or sesame oil. They are also very tasty served cold in a vinaigrette.

Snow peas

Sugar snap peas

Sugar Snap Pea

The sugar snap pea *(Pisum sativum var. axiphium)* is a relatively new variety of edible-podded pea. It has a thicker pod than the snow pea with well developed seeds. The sugar snap pea has a sweet flavor. Select; prepare and cook like snow peas, see opposite page.

Asparagus Pea

The asparagus pea *(Lotus tetragonolobus)*, or winged pea is not a true pea but, like the snow pea is eaten pod and all. It has a mild, delicate asparagus flavor. The pods should be picked when very young. Prepare and cook like snow peas, see opposite page.

Fava Bean

The fava bean *(Vicia faba)* is one of the oldest of cultivated vegetables and is thought to have come from the East, although its exact origin is obscure. Fava beans have been eaten for centuries; fortunately the modern varieties are a great improvement on the tough bean of times past.

They grow in large thick pods with a soft furry lining and are available from mid-spring through to late summer. Buy soft, tender, bright green pods that are not too large and puffy. Best used fresh, they may be stored in a plastic bag in the crisper drawer of the refrigerator up to two days.

Preparation & Cooking
Unless very young and tender, fava beans need shelling. Once the beans are larger than a big pea, their skins are coarse and tough and should also be removed. Skin beans raw or after cooking, when cool enough to handle. Slit the skin along the indented edge of the bean, then squeeze to remove the bean.

To cook, simmer in just enough lightly salted water to cover, with butter added, eight to ten minutes or until tender.

Serving Suggestions
Toss and heat cooked, drained fava beans in garlic butter or cream and fresh herbs, or serve with a parsley or cheese sauce.

A puree of fava beans, mixed with butter and cream, makes a delicious accompaniment for ham, or it may be turned into a rich soup with a cheese topping, see page 77.

For a salad, drain cooked fava beans and toss while still hot in a well-seasoned vinaigrette; chill before serving. If desired, cool, then mix into a lemon mayonnaise or serve in a potato salad, flavored with finely grated lemon peel.

Runner Bean

The bean *(Phaseolus coccineus)*, native to South America, was brought to Britain in the early 17th century. For many years, the beans were grown for their beauty as an ornamental plant, not as a vegetable!

Runner beans have large, flat bright green succulent pods which need stringing before cooking. They are widely grown by keen gardeners.

Available from mid-summer until the beginning of autumn, fresh beans should snap in half when bent. They will keep well in a plastic bag in the crisper drawer of the refrigerator two to three days.

Preparation & Cooking
Trim and string young beans; more mature beans are best thinly pared all the way around to avoid any stringiness. Cut in thin slices or short diagonal lengths or shell mature beans. Cook in boiling salted water five to twelve minutes, until tender, according to size and age. Or steam, allowing a few minutes extra cooking. Drain well and return to pan over low heat for a few seconds to dry off.

Serving Suggestions
The simplest way to enjoy these beans is to add salt and pepper to taste and butter, or a spoonful or two of cream, and heat through gently, tossing until beans are evenly coated. These beans are also good cooked *à la grecque,* or blanched and stir-fried.

They are delicious in salads, relishes and pickles, and can be added with other vegetables to hot soups or rice or pasta mixtures.

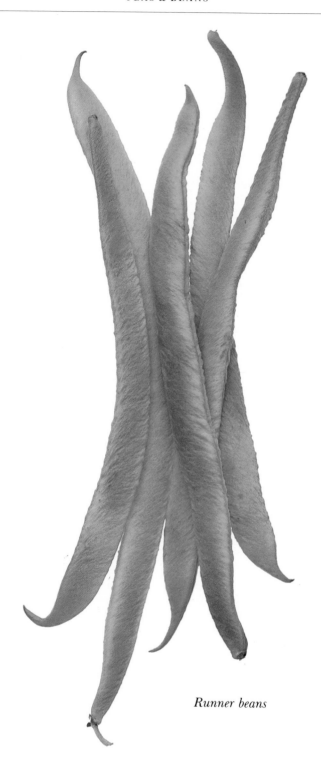

Runner beans

Lima Bean

The lima bean *(Phaseolus lunatus)* is native to Lima, Peru. Lima beans are normally found fresh only in the tropical areas where they grow.

These beans are flat and kidney-shaped. They are shelled and cooked as fava beans, see opposite page. They are available frozen, dried and canned.

Edible-Pod Bean

The edible-pod bean *(Phaseolus vulgaris)*, also known as the French bean, haricot vert, green bean and string bean, originated in Central and South America. It arrived in Europe early in the 16th century. There are numerous varieties; most of the common ones have slender green pods, tapering to a small tail. The Dwarf bean and the Bobbi bean varieties are thicker though similar in shape. Most of these beans are stringless when young.

Edible-pod beans are more or less available all year, but can be expensive in winter. Buy beans of the same size and thickness to ensure even cooking; they should be fresh enough to snap in half. If not using immediately, store in the crisper drawer of the refrigerator two to three days.

Preparation & Cooking
Trim and string beans, if necessary. Drop into boiling salted water, cover and cook about five minutes or until tender-crisp, depending on size. Or steam 10 to 12 minutes, if desired. Drain, return to pan over low heat for a few minutes to dry off. If serving cold, drain and plunge beans into cold water, then drain again—this helps preserve a good color.

Serving Suggestions
Cold, cooked beans are excellent dressed with a herbed vinaigrette and served as a first course, or added to salads, such as Salade Niçoise—a traditional favorite.

Sauté hot beans with small slivers of bacon and crushed garlic until bacon is crisp and golden. Toss hot beans in melted butter and seasonings, then sprinkle liberally with grated Parmesan cheese and crisp buttery crumbs. Delicious too, sautéed with button mushrooms and topped with toasted almonds. Try them in a garlicky tomato sauce, sprinkled with mozzarella cheese and broiled. Or sauté in olive oil with slivers of peeled tomato and red bell pepper and serve with grilled steaks.

Bean Sprout

The mung bean *(Phaseolus mungo)* is the bean most commonly used for producing bean sprouts, although a number of other beans are also used for the same purpose. The mung bean is native to India, where the beans (not the shoots) are cooked and pureed to provide a staple food.

Bean sprouts are the young, tender shoots of the bean and are very crisp and nutritious. They can be grown year-round and are fun and simple to grow at home.

At one time, bean sprouts were rather hard to find—Chinese supermarkets were about the only places selling them. Now, however, they are widely available from supermarkets and produce markets, sold loose or in packages. They are at their best when fresh, but may be kept 24 hours in the refrigerator.

Preparation & Cooking
Bean sprouts only need washing before using. If desired, bean sprouts can be blanched before use. Cover with boiling water and leave 30 to 45 seconds. (They will still be crisp.) Drain well, then use as needed.

Serving Suggestions
Raw bean sprouts add crunchiness and an interesting flavor to salads and make a welcome change in sandwich fillings.

Stir-frying is a good way of cooking bean sprouts, as they must be cooked quickly to enjoy their crispness and delicate flavor. Try them stir-fried or flavored with a little ginger and sprinkled with soy sauce and sesame oil, or combined with other ingredients.

Add bean sprouts to clear soups a minute or two before serving. Or make into fritters; fold bean sprouts into a thick, garlicky batter and deep-fry briefly until golden. Serve hot with soy or chili sauce.

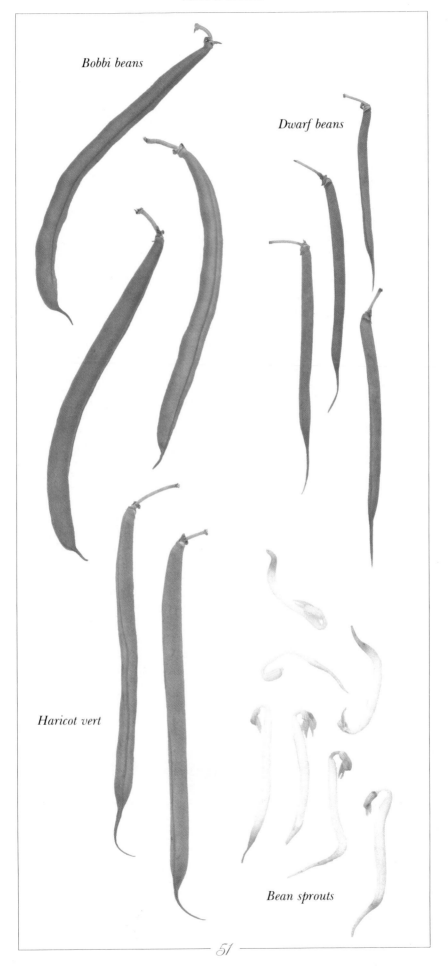

Bobbi beans

Dwarf beans

Haricot vert

Bean sprouts

Asparagus

Asparagus (*Asparagus officinalis*) is a member of the lily family, the edible parts being the immature shoots of the tuberous root. It is thought to have originated in the eastern Mediterranean and Asia Minor and was a favorite with the ancient Greeks and Romans.

The home-grown asparagus season is very short in the northern hemisphere—mid-spring to early summer. Imported asparagus is in stores throughout the year.

Asparagus is a choice but expensive vegetable, sold loose or in bundles, usually graded according to thickness of stems. It can be thick or thin, light- or dark-green, and sometimes green and purple. The top grade has fat tender stalks; the thinner variety is less expensive and still very good to eat.

Buying & Storing
When selecting asparagus, look for crisp stalks and tight, plump well formed buds—avoid woody and dry stems. Asparagus is best eaten soon after purchase as it is very perishable. It will keep in the crisper drawer of the refrigerator up to two days (do not wash first).

Preparation & Cooking
Fresh young asparagus is tender for most of its length. Bend each stem until it snaps—the break will come at the point where the stem begins to toughen. Young green spears need only trimming at the cut end. Thicker spears need trimming where the stalk begins to feel tough: using a vegetable peeler, shave off the woody parts at the cut end, then trim to make all the same length. Rinse stalks in cold water and tie in bunches of about 12 with tips level.

The stalks take longer to cook than the tips; to cook successfully, they should stand upright in enough simmering salted water to reach two-thirds up the stems. The tougher stalks boil while the tender tips steam more gently. Improvise with a domed cover of foil if you haven't a deep enough saucepan. An asparagus pan, specificially designed for the job, is ideal. It is tall, narrow and lined with a basket or perforated inner container which can be lifted out.

Cooking time varies according to the thickness and quality of asparagus. Allow 8 to 12 minutes for tender young spears; 12 to 20 minutes for larger spears. Asparagus should be tender-crisp when ready (never floppy). Test by spearing a stalk with the point of a sharp knife. Drain thoroughly, lift asparagus from pan, cut string and place asparagus on a clean folded towel a few seconds to absorb moisture.

Serving Suggestions
Asparagus is delicious served hot, warm or cold. It's easier to hold in the fingers for dipping into sauces. Serve it with melted butter flavored with lemon juice and pepper, or with a rich hollandaise or mousseline sauce.

Try asparagus coated with a Gruyère sauce and grilled until golden, or served on top creamy scrambled eggs. Delicious too, stir-fried, pureed in a cream soup, in mousses, or used as an attractive open sandwich topping or vol-au-vent filling for buffets.

Cardoon

Cardoon (*Cynara cardunculus*), a native of the Mediterranean region, was a popular vegetable in Britain and France in the 17th and 18th centuries. It is closely related to the globe artichoke and is similar in flavor, but cardoon is cultivated for its leafy stalks, which are blanched (just like celery) during growing.

Cardoon is in season during autumn and early winter. Look for firm, fresh, translucent stalks. Washed and trimmed, it will keep well in a plastic bag in the refrigerator up to five days.

Preparation & Cooking
Trim off root end, discard tough outer stems and leaves and cut prick-

Asparagus

Sprue asparagus

Purple-tinged asparagus

les from inner stalks. Separate stalks and heart; cut stalks in lengths.

To eat raw, remove strings and inner white skin from stalks and slice heart thinly. Rub with a cut lemon to prevent discoloration (or place in water with lemon juice added); pat dry before serving.

Cook cardoon in simmering water 25 to 30 minutes, or braise in a moderate oven 1-1/4 hours.

Serving Suggestions

Eat stalks and heart raw, like celery, with dips such as *aïoli*, or slice into salads.

Enjoy cardoons hot with melted butter, cheese or cream sauce. Also extremely good tossed in a mixture of butter, cream and grated Parmesan cheese. The hearts are delicious, boiled until tender, then served cold in mayonnaise or vinaigrette as a first course.

Celery

Celery (*Apium graveolens* var. *dulce*) is native to Europe. It was held in high regard, both as a food and medicinally, by the Ancient Greeks, Romans and Egyptians. However, the crisp, succulent celery we know today is the result of 16th century Italian gardeners, who developed it from the bitter-tasting weed of years ago.

Celery is available in stores all year. There are many varieties, including the white (blanched) and light- to dark-green types. The green types are becoming more popular for their flavor and lack of stringiness.

Buying & Storing
Choose compact heads with firm sticks and plump bottoms. Leaves should be brightly colored and fresh looking. Store unwashed celery, loosely wrapped, in the crisper drawer of the refrigerator up to five days. To crisp and revive wilted celery, soak in ice cold water one hour before serving.

Preparation & Cooking
Trim off bottom and separate stalks. Scrub, rinse clean and remove leaves and any strings.

To prepare celery hearts, break off outer stalks, leaving a crisp cluster of smaller, tender, tightly packed stalks about two inches thick. Cut off tops to give pieces measuring about six inches in length. Leave whole or cut in half lengthwise and wash well. Cook in boiling salted water about 20 minutes until tender, or steam or braise allowing a little longer.

Serving Suggestions
Tender, young celery is best eaten raw in salads or included in crudités with a selection of dips. Pieces of celery are delicious stuffed with a filling, such as cream cheese and walnuts or taramasalata.

Celery also adds flavor and interest to casseroles, stuffings, rice and pasta dishes. Stir-frying is a quick way to cook thinly sliced celery and one which preserves its color, flavor and texture. Try sprinkling with toasted cashews and a little sesame oil before serving.

Celery hearts, blanched in boiling water ten minutes, then braised in stock on a bed of onions and bacon, make a good accompaniment. Or braise, then bake with a cheese or tomato sauce.

Sweet Fennel

Sweet fennel (*Foeniculum vulgare* var. *dulce*), also known as Florentine or Florence fennel, is a native of the Mediterranean region. It is a bulbous-shaped vegetable with a swollen, ribbed leaf bottom (also called a bulb or head). The texture is crisp with a flavor of aniseed. It is delicious served raw or cooked.

Fennel is available all year. Buy bulbs which are well-rounded in shape and pale-green to white in color—avoid any which are dark-green. They will keep up to five days in a plastic bag in the refrigerator.

Preparation & Cooking
If the bulb has leafy fronds at the top, save these for garnishing or adding to salads. Trim bottom, cut off thin ends of stalks, then halve, quarter, slice or chop, as required.

Cook in boiling salted water about 15 minutes until tender but still crisp. Or steam, braise or sauté in butter.

Serving Suggestions
Fennel is extremely good teamed with fish and shellfish. Try it raw or parboiled and grated in seafood cocktails, or add to a salad and toss in a garlicky vinaigrette or mayonnaise. It is also good simmered in lightly salted water until just tender, then served drizzled with melted herb butter; tossed in cream; or sprinkled with lemon juice and pepper. Baked Italian-style, see page 94, or cooked *à la grecque*, fennel is equally good.

Green celery

White celery

Sweet fennel

Seakale

Seakale *(Crambe maritima)* is native to Britain, where it grows wild along the coasts, and to most coastal regions of western Europe. It has been eaten for centuries.

Preparation & Cooking
Wash thoroughly and trim off earthy stalks. The young leaves may be left on or trimmed, if desired, and used in salads. Tie the stalks in bunches and simmer, on their sides, in salted water or chicken stock about 25 minutes, until tender; steam if preferred. Take care not to overcook this vegetable or it will toughen. Drain well.

Serving Suggestions
The leaves of seakale are delicious shredded or chopped into salads or they may be cooked like spinach, see page 20.

Enjoy seakale stalks in the same way as you would asparagus spears: hot with a melted butter and lemon sauce, hollandaise or a creamy béchamel. For an accompaniment, arrange partially cooked stalks in an ovenproof dish, coat with cheese sauce, grated cheese and crumbs and bake until golden-brown.

Mushroom

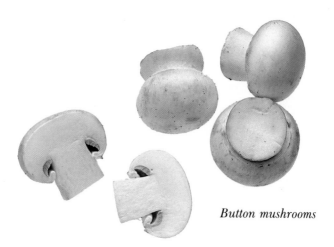

Button mushrooms

Mushrooms have been around for thousands of years, but it was less than three centuries ago that man discovered how to cultivate this delicious edible fungi. The mushroom cultivated in the West *(Agaricus bisporus)* is closely related to the field mushroom *(Agaricus campestris)*. Cultivated mushrooms ara available all year-round.

Button mushrooms are small, white and tightly closed, with a delicate flavor.

Cup and **open cup-mushrooms** are button types which have been left to grow larger. When still closed underneath (so that the gills cannot be seen) they are known as cups, but when the white skin round the stalk breaks away exposing the gills, they become open cups. Both types have fuller flavor than the button type.

Open mushrooms are more mature, the next stage in growth from cup and open cup.

Flat mushrooms are fully matured, with darker gills. Both open and flat types have a rich flavor.

Oyster mushrooms and **Chestnut browns** are relatively new cultivated varieties.

Buying & Storing

Provided mushrooms are fresh when purchased, they store well (in the carton or paper bag in which they were bought) in the refrigerator two to three days. Always remove mushrooms from plastic bags to prevent them becoming sticky.

Preparation & Cooking

There is no need to peel cultivated mushrooms, whatever their size—unless you prefer. A wipe with a clean damp cloth to remove dirt should be sufficient. For a large quantity, place in a colander and rinse very quickly under cold running water, then dry on paper towels. Trim stalk ends.

Mushrooms can be left whole, quartered, sliced or chopped, according to recipe. The stalks need to be removed from large flat types for grilling or stuffing. Mushrooms are naturally tender, so they require little cooking.

Serving Suggestions

Mushrooms are good eaten raw in salads or served with dips as crudités. They are also delicious marinated in a lemony vinaigrette, as a first course. Large flat mushrooms, piled high with a tasty stuffing and grilled or baked, make a popular starter.

Mushrooms are delicious in quiches or cooked *à la grecque* with tomatoes, herbs and garlic. Serve sautéed mushrooms—on their own or mixed into a rich cream sauce—on toast as a tasty snack. Button mushrooms lend their delicate flavor to sauces and soups; they are especially good with sherry or wine. Use the button variety too in kabobs, or try them dipped into batter and deep-fried until golden, see page 89.

Cup mushrooms

Open-cup mushrooms

Flat mushrooms

Oyster mushrooms

Chestnut-brown mushrooms

Tomato

Green-house tomato

Yellow green-house tomato

The tomato (*Lycopersicon esculentum*) is actually a fruit, but is used as a vegetable. It originated in South America and arrived in Europe less than four centuries ago. At first, tomatoes were grown simply as decorative garden plants, as they were considered dangerous to eat, being related to poisonous plants of the *Solanaceae* family, including Deadly Nightshade.

Tomatoes are available all year. Home-grown ones are available from mid-spring through summer. There are many interesting varieties from which to choose.

The very smallest is the *cherry tomato*—it's tiny, sweet, crisp and juicy. *Plum (Roma) tomatoes* are elongated. They are available fresh and are familiar in peeled and canned form. *Beefsteak tomatoes* are large and beefy and extremely tasty. Yellow tomato varieties are becoming more widely available.

Buying & Storing
Choose firm tomatoes—ripe if to be eaten immediately—or a little underripe for eating in a few days. The flavor is better if tomatoes are not refrigerated.

Preparation
Many recipes require tomatoes to be peeled and seeded. To do this, place tomatoes in a bowl and cover with boiling water. Let stand 30 to 60 seconds, according to ripeness, then drain and peel. To seed tomatoes, cut in half or quarters and, using a teaspoon, scoop out seeds.

To make tomato roses, using a sharp knife, pare away peel in a spiral, then coil it around your finger to form a rose shape. To make V-cut tomatoes, see page 103.

Serving Suggestions
Thinly sliced tomatoes, sprinkled with olive or walnut oil and chopped basil, make a wonderful side salad; add slices of mozzarella cheese for a delicious first course. Stuff tomatoes with various fillings, such as avocado and crab, taramasalata or herbed cream cheese.

Cooked tomatoes make popular accompaniments: try halved tomatoes topped with garlic-buttered crumbs and a curled anchovy, baked until golden. The large beefsteak types are excellent for stuffing and baking, to serve hot or cold.

Use tomatoes to make soups such as refreshing Gazpacho and tomato and basil soup. Tomatoes make excellent sauces and dips for serving hot and cold. They are of course indispensable in pizza toppings, ratatouille and many fillings for pancakes, pies and quiches. Unripe green tomatoes make marvelous pickles and chutneys.

Beefsteak tomato

Plum (Roma) tomatoes

Yellow pear tomato

Cherry tomatoes

Squash

Squash (*Cucurbitaceae*), along with other members of the family such as pumpkin and marrow, are native to the Americas and have been grown for thousands of years. The term squash comes from the American-Indian *askootasquash*.

The squash family is a rather confusing one with squash, pumpkin and marrow being varieties of a single species. To simplify matters, the more well known varieties—namely pumpkin, zucchini and vegetable marrow—have individual entries. Most of the other types available can be classified as summer or winter squash.

Summer squash: These are usually thin-skinned, immature and tender and do not need peeling. Summer squash (*Cucurbita pepo*) come in a range of interesting shapes and colors and include the orange, scalloped-shaped *cymling;* light- or dark-green *pattypan;* pale-green pear-shaped *chayote* (choko, or christophene) which contains an edible seed with a nutty flavor; pale-green, yellow or white *custard marrow;* and the orange or yellow *crookneck.*

Winter squash: These are more mature and generally larger than summer varieties. They have hard skins, which may or may not be peeled before cooking, according to type and recipe. Varieties of winter squash (*Cucurbita maxima*) include the elongated, pear-shaped yellow *butternut;* dark-green *acorn squash;* the large green *hubbard;* the flattish round Japanese *butterball;* and the melon-shaped, yellow *spaghetti squash.* The elongated green *bitter gourd (Momordica charantia)* is an Indian squash, albeit from another family.

Buying & Storing
You will find a variety of squash available throughout the year in ethnic markets and supermarkets. Look for firm squash with unblemished skins.

Summer squash can be stored in the crisper drawer of the refrigerator several days or longer.

Winter squash keep well several weeks or even months, stored in a cool dry place.

Preparation & Cooking
Trim top and stem ends of summer squash, then leave whole, halve or quarter, slice, dice or cut in chunks, as required. Summer squash may be cooked in the same ways as zucchini.

Winter squash are often halved, or cut in wedges, seeded and baked with a tasty filling. They may also be sliced, diced or cut in chunks and steamed, boiled or roasted until tender. Spaghetti squash is boiled whole in its skin, then halved and the tangled fibers scooped out before serving.

Serving Suggestions
Summer squash are delicious steamed and pureed with butter, cream and seasonings, or served sautéed and sprinkled with finely grated orange peel, cinnamon-flavored sugar, or crisp crumbled bacon and chives. Enjoy them stuffed and baked with a tasty meat or spiced lentil filling. Or coat slices in batter or egg and crumbs and deep-fry as an unusual accompaniment. Diced summer squash is also good added to casseroles and pot roasts towards the end of cooking. Chayotes are delicious stuffed and baked, see page 92, or try them steamed or boiled until almost tender, then sautéed in garlic butter.

Serve slices of steamed winter squash coated with garlicky tomato sauce and cheese, or dice and add to casseroles and curries. Parboiled portions of winter squash are good baked around a roast, or steamed until tender and pureed with butter and spices. Delicious too, in soups, preserves and pickles.

Serve spaghetti squash hot with melted butter, a rich bolognese sauce, or with cream herbs and cheese. It is also good served cold with a tangy vinaigrette.

Butternut squash

Chayote squash

Custard marrow squash

Acorn squash

Butterball squash

Spaghetti squash

Bitter gourds

Pumpkin

The pumpkin *(Cucurbita pepo)* has been grown in the Americas for thousands of years; it reached Europe comparatively recently. It is closely related to squash, marrow and zucchini.

Pumpkins come in a range of shapes with hard, colorful bright orange, green or beige skins; they are all similar in flavor.

Pumpkins are available virtually all year, but especially at Halloween. They are usually rather large, but are often sold cut in smaller pieces. Whole pumpkins store well in a cool dry place several weeks; cut portions, covered in plastic wrap, keep successfully in the refrigerator up to one week.

Preparation & Cooking
Pumpkins need cutting in smaller pieces for easy handling. Cut away skin, remove seeds, then slice, dice or cut pulp in chunky pieces, as required. Do not discard the seeds. Roasted and salted, they make a delicious snack; sprinkle over dishes as a garnish, too.

Pumpkin may be steamed, boiled and baked. It may also be steamed in wedges and the pulp scraped away from the skin after cooking.

Serving Suggestions
The most famous use must be pumpkin pie—a tasty mixture of pumpkin puree, spices and cream, served in a pastry shell. On the savory side, pumpkin is excellent pureed in soups, or parboiled and baked around a roast, like potatoes. Mashed pumpkin, enriched with butter and flavored with cinnamon, also makes an unusually good accompaniment. Or try pumpkin diced and sautéed and drizzled with melted butter, honey or maple syrup.

Vegetable Marrow

The vegetable marrow *(Cucurbita pepe ovifera)* is a British vegetable. It is closely related to the squash, pumpkin and zucchini.

Marrows are available during summer to early autumn. They vary from light- to dark-green and/or yellow and are most often striped. Select firm, heavy, smallish marrows as these have plenty of flavor; the large ones can be rather flavorless. Whole marrows will store well in a cool, dry place as long as a month or so.

Preparation & Cooking
When really young and tender, marrows need not be peeled—trim ends, cut in pieces and cook as you would zucchini. For larger marrows, trim off ends and peel thinly, then slice, cut in halves or rings and remove seeds and surrounding fibers.

Marrow is delicious baked, steamed, braised or sautéed. Take care not to overcook this vegetable or it becomes mushy and tasteless. It is best when just tender, but still with a bite.

Serving Suggestions
Stuffed marrow is a great favorite: cut lengthwise in half or in chunky rings, fill with a good flavorful mixture, sprinkle with cheesy crumbs and bake until just tender. Or try chunky pieces of marrow basted and baked around a roast (add towards the end of cooking time to prevent overcooking). Slices of marrow steamed and served in a creamy garlicky sauce make an excellent accompaniment, or bake in buttered foil to retain the juices and sprinkle with fresh herbs just before serving. Diced marrow, sautéed in clarified butter and spiced with ground cumin or coriander, is delicious.

Try cream of marrow soup, or perhaps a dish of marrow *au gratin*. Marrow is also an excellent vegetable for making chutneys and delicious marrow and ginger jam.

Pumpkin

Green-striped marrow

Yellow-striped marrow

Spherical Italian zucchini

Dark-green zucchini

Striped zucchini

Yellow zucchini

Zucchini

The zucchini *(Cucurbita pepo)*, closely related to squash, is a distinct variety of small vegetable marrow, picked when four to six inches long.

Zucchini is available all year. The skin may be yellow, pale- or dark-green, or striped. Most varieties are oblong in shape, but a spherical Italian zucchini is available.

Buying & Storing
Zucchini is at its best when small. The skin should be smooth and glossy, and the vegetable should feel firm and crisp. Best eaten fresh, although they will keep in the crisper drawer of the refrigerator two to three days.

Preparation & Cooking
Trim off ends but do not peel. Zucchini can be eaten raw, or cooked whole, sliced or chopped. It may be steamed, sautéed in butter, dipped into batter or egg and bread crumbs and fried, or stuffed and baked. Take care not to overcook—this vegetable is best when tender, but still crisp.

Serving Suggestions
Diced or thinly sliced raw zucchini is refreshing in salads. Try grated raw zucchini and carrot tossed in a herbed French dressing and served chilled in crisp radicchio cups.

Cut in half, or with a lengthwise slice removed, and partially hollowed out, zucchini is delicious filled with tasty stuffings and served hot or cold. Quartered lengthwise, dipped into a light batter or egg and crumbs and deep-fried, it is very good served hot with a selection of tasty dips, or as an accompaniment to grilled steaks. Delicious too, in ratatouille; served sweet and sour style; or added to stir-fry dishes.

Cucumber

The cucumber *(Cucumis sativus)* was one of the earliest cultivated vegetables, and is thought to be native to India.

There are two basic types of cucumber: the long, thin, smooth-skinned, green hot-house variety; (Continental cucumber); and the rough-skinned, thicker, shorter ridge cucumber—grown outdoors on raised ridges of soil. Mini varieties are available.

Buying & Storing

Available all-year round, choose cucumbers that look fresh and feel firm, particularly at the stem end. Store in the crisper drawer of the refrigerator several days (remove tight plastic wrappings).

Ridge cucumbers are better peeled, but only peel the hot-house type if the skin is tough or the cucumber is to be cooked. Using a canelle knife, cut thin channels in the skin for attractive slices. Cut off ends as these are bitter. Cucumber is often de-gorged to remove excess moisture before use, see eggplant, page 66.

Serving Suggestions

Cucumber is probably best enjoyed in salads and sandwiches or, cut in sticks as a crudité for dunking into dips. Hollowed-out cucumber rings, filled with cream cheese, pâté or egg and shrimp mayonnaise, are ideal buffet fare. Slices or twists of cucumber make pretty garnishes.

Use cucumber to make pickles and relishes, or grate or dice and mix with yogurt, garlic and perhaps mint, to serve as a refreshing side dish with kabobs and curries.

Cooked cucumber is also good. Fill hollowed-out cucumber halves with tasty mixtures, sprinkle with cheese and bake until tender. Or using a melon baller, cut in cubes or balls. Steam 15 minutes, then toss in melted butter or dairy sour cream and serve as an accompaniment.

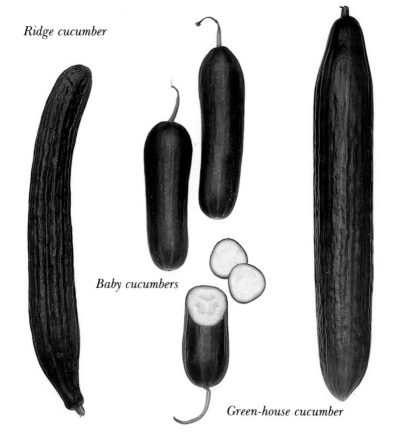

Ridge cucumber

Baby cucumbers

Green-house cucumber

Eggplant

The eggplant (*Solanum melongena* var. *esculentum*) is a tropical vegetable fruit native to southern Asia. It is known as *brinjal* in India, *melanzane* in Italy. Eggplants vary in shape—some being long and thin, others pear-shaped or round. Miniature varieties are available. Skin color varies too—most are purply-black but they can also be yellow-white.

Buying & Storing
Available all year, buy those which are firm, shiny and smooth. They will keep up to three days in the crisper drawer of the refrigerator.

Preparation & Cooking
Trim off the leafy end, but do not remove skin. Use a stainless steel knife when preparing to prevent pulp turning black. Slice, chop or dice, or halve and hollow out for stuffing.

As eggplants absorb a lot of oil when fried, they can be degorged beforehand to reduce this; layer prepared vegetable in a colander with salt, cover with a weighted plate and let drain 30 minutes. Rinse and pat dry.

Eggplants can be baked, stuffed, pureed, grilled, shallow or deep-fried and braised. To fry slices, dust with seasoned flour, then fry in olive oil two to three minutes on each side. To grill slices, brush with oil and grill three to four minutes each side.

To puree for making dips and pâtés, bake at 400F (205C) 45 minutes or until soft and blackened, then halve and scoop out the pulp.

To stuff an eggplant, cut in half lengthwise or cut a slice off one long side. Hollow out the center, leaving a one-inch border. Add the removed pulp (degorged, if desired) to the other filling ingredients, spoon into the shells and bake until tender. Serve hot or cold, depending on filling.

Serving Suggestions
Ratatouille is a favorite—as a starter or accompaniment—or make Ratatouille Cheese Gougère, see page 98. Braised eggplant, served with a bowl of thick creamy yogurt, is very good; spice Indian-style, if desired.

Use pureed eggplant to make a tasty dip; flavor with garlic and tahini, and serve with warm pita bread; or turn into a tasty hot soufflé.

Slices or sticks of eggplant, dipped into a batter or egg and bread crumbs and deep-fried, are delicious served hot, sprinkled with grated Parmesan cheese.

Okra

Okra (*Hibiscus esculentus*) came originally from Africa and is now grown in many tropical and subtropical areas. Also known as ladies' fingers, okra is a long pointed green pod.

Buying & Storing
Okra is widely available throughout the year. Look for bright, fresh green pods about four inches long that feel firm and crisp. Avoid any blemished pods. Okra may be stored in a plastic bag in the crisper drawer of the refrigerator two to three days.

Preparation & Cooking
Okra may be left whole, sliced or cut in pieces. When cooked for any length of time, it secretes a glutinous substance which acts as a thickener for soups and stews. This is essential for the thick Creole-style Gumbo.

Trim okra to remove the stalk, if desired, taking care not to cut off too much of the conical cap or it will become sticky during cooking. Simmer in salted water for five minutes until tender-crisp; steam 10 to 15 minutes; or sauté in butter or oil for five to ten minutes, depending on size. Rapid and short cooking is best for okra, unless otherwise stated in a recipe, as overcooking causes it to be slimy.

Serving Suggestions
If the pods are very small, they may be sliced and served raw in dressed salads. Okra is delicious sautéed with

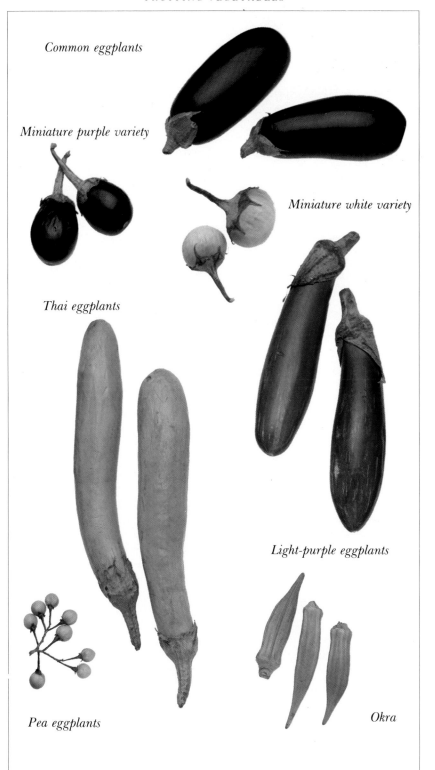

Common eggplants

Miniature purple variety

Miniature white variety

Thai eggplants

Light-purple eggplants

Pea eggplants

Okra

onions, garlic and tomatoes as an un- usual first course. Sprinkled with cheese and buttered crumbs and broiled, it becomes a tasty lunch or supper dish. Try it boiled or steamed and served with lemony butter to eat with the fingers as you would aspar- agus spears—simple but very good.

As an accompaniment, sauté okra with diced eggplant, spiced with on- ions, garlic, coriander and turmeric; spiced this way it is equally good stirred into hot rice dishes. Okra also makes a delicious pickle.

Globe artichoke

Young globe artichoke

Globe Artichoke

The globe artichoke *(Cynara scolymus)* originally came from the Mediterranean. Globe artichokes are unopened thistle heads and have no connection with Jerusalem artichokes. Globe artichokes are at their most plentiful during spring and summer. Look for the very small and immature flower buds, picked before the chokes develop; these are tender enough to be eaten whole.

Buying & Storing
Choose heavy artichokes that feel thick and solid with tightly-packed leaves. They are best eaten when fresh, although they will store in a plastic bag in the refrigerator two to three days.

Preparation & Cooking
The small, tender flower buds need only a trim at the stem end and a good washing to eat. Cook in boiling salted water, or dry white wine flavored with olive oil and herbs, until just tender. Drain and serve hot or cold.

For a large artichoke heart, trim stalk level with bottom and remove any damaged outer leaves. Trim outer leaves, if desired; wash well.

Cook in boiling salted water with a slice of lemon added 30 to 45 minutes, until tender. To test, lift from pan and pull off one of the outer leaves—if it comes away easily it is cooked. Drain upside down in a colander. Serve artichoke as it is or with the choke removed, see page 80.

Serving Suggestions
To eat an artichoke, pull off one leaf at a time, dip the tender succulent end into a sauce and nibble off the soft part with your teeth. Discard the rest of the leaf (provide finger bowls and plates for dicarded leaves). The heart is then eaten with a knife and fork, provided the choke has been removed.

Serve artichokes hot with melted butter, lemon butter or hollandaise, or cold with vinaigrette, *aïoli* or a rich garlicky tomato sauce. Served cold, they are also extremely good filled with a pâté or seafood mixture.

Artichoke hearts are excellent blanched and sautéed in butter or dipped into egg and bread crumbs and deep-fried. They are delicious, too, added to salads.

Corn

Corn *(Zea mays)*, also known as Indian corn, is a type of maize native to Central America, where it has been grown for over 5,000 years.

Corn-on-the-cob is available during summer and autumn. Dwarf (baby) corn is available in the summer. Canned dwarf corn is available all year.

Buying & Storing
Select corn that is full and plump with bright, creamy colored kernels, not dark-yellow as this is a sign of age. If fresh and tender, a kernel of corn exudes a milky liquid when split open. Eat corn-on-the-cob fresh or keep one to two days, wrapped in a plastic bag in the refrigerator. Dwarf corn keeps well in the crisper drawer of the refrigerator several days.

Preparation & Cooking
Trim away outer leaves, silky threads and stalks from corn-on-the-cob and wash thoroughly. Cook in boiling *unsalted* water five to eight minutes for freshly picked corn, 15 to 20 minutes if older. Add a pinch of sugar to the water, if desired. Salt and overcooking both toughen corn.

Corn-on-the-cob may also be barbecued or grilled eight to ten minutes; brush liberally with butter and turn frequently. If the corn is older, boil 10 minutes first. Or, brush corn with butter, wrap in foil and bake at 350F (175C) 30 minutes.

To remove the kernels from the cob, hold the cob firmly, stalk-end down on a flat surface. Using a sharp knife, make downward strokes to cut away the kernels. Cook these in boiling *unsalted* water six to eight minutes, or steam 10 to 15 minutes.

Dwarf corn may be eaten raw or cooked. Simply wash and serve raw, or boil, steam or stir-fry briefly until tender-crisp.

Serving Suggestions
Very fresh, tender young kernels are delicious added raw to salads or use dwarf corn-on-the-cob as dipping sticks with *aïoli.* Stir kernels into a thick batter and fry to make fritters. Make into a creamy soup or add to a thick, chunky fish chowder. Mix kernels into stir-fry dishes, savory rice and pasta dishes.

Whole corn is best served with plenty of melted butter and freshly ground pepper. Parboiled corn-on-the-cob, cut in chunky slices, makes an attractive addition to kabobs.

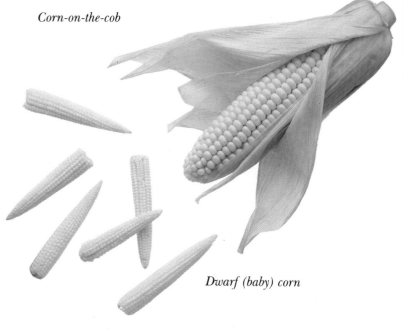

Corn-on-the-cob

Dwarf (baby) corn

Avocado

Fuerte

The avocado is actually a fruit (belonging to the genus *Persea*). It is included here because it is more often served as a vegetable. For centuries is has been cultivated and eaten in its native South America; indeed, its name is derived from the Aztec *ahuacet.* Avocados are now grown in most tropical countries and are popular worldwide. Believe it or not, there are over 500 varieties.

The most popular varieties are *Egginger,* oblong with bright, shiny, smooth green skin; *Hass,* a purply black-skinned variety; *Fuerte,* oblong with dark-green, slightly rough skin; and *Habal,* a large round fruit with a large seed. There is also now a tiny *Cocktail* avocado available which has no seed.

Buying & Storing
Avocados are in stores all year-round. To enjoy them, they must be perfectly ripe. You can't assess ripeness by looking at the skin, so cradle the fruit in the palm of your hand—it should yield slightly all over to gentle pressure. Store ripe avocados in the crisper drawer of the refrigerator up to three days. Cut avocados, sprinkled with lemon juice and with their seed still in, keep up to 24 hours, in the refrigerator, wrapped in plastic wrap.

To speed ripening, place avocados in a bowl in a warm room.

Preparation
To open an avocado, cut in half lengthwise through to the seed, using a stainless steel knife. Separate in half by carefully rotating each half in opposite directions. Remove seed and rub cut surfaces with lemon juice to prevent discoloration. To slice, peel, place cut-side down and slice lengthwise or crosswise, if desired.

Serving Suggestions
As starters, avocados are always popular halved, seeded and filled with a vinaigrette or shrimp mixture. For a change, fill the cavities with Roquefort mayonnaise or flaked crabmeat marinated in lemon juice. Avocado and grapefruit slices complement each other perfectly as a delicate first course.

Pureed avocado pulp makes refreshing and stylish chilled soups, and delicious dips, such as spicy Mexican guacamole.

The nutty, delicate flavor and succulent texture of avocados makes them ideal to include in salads: try avocado with bacon and spinach, or chicken and avocado salad.

Avocados may also be baked with a savory filling—a creamy seafood mixture is particularly good. Some folks claim that the delicate flavor of avocado is not as good hot.

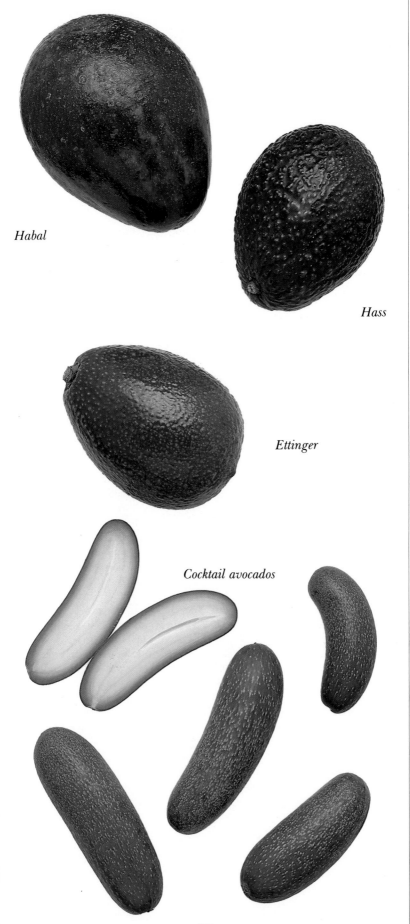

Habal

Hass

Ettinger

Cocktail avocados

Pepper

There are many varieties of pepper, but the two most important species are the bell pepper *(Capsicum annuum)* and the chile pepper *(Capsicum frutescens)*. Both are native to the West Indies and tropical America.

BELL PEPPER

Bell peppers come in a range of colors and sizes. The crisp green pepper is the unripe fruit which, as it matures, turns red or yellow (according to variety). White, brown and purple-black peppers are also available, but not as widely as the green, yellow and red types.

Flavor and texture of the various colored bell peppers varies slightly; green are crisp and mildly spicy; yellow ones are crisp and slightly sweeter; red peppers are softer in texture with the sweetest flavor of all. The white and purple-black varieties are similar to green bell peppers. The bell-shaped Scotch bonnets are spicy.

It is the red bell pepper which is dried and ground to make paprika. Canned red bell peppers are called pimentos.

CHILE PEPPER

The chile pepper is much smaller than the bell pepper and is generally used as a flavoring rather than a vegetable. Chiles vary in size, shape and heat factor according to ripeness, but they are always hot and fiery, so be warned!

Fresh chiles are available green, yellow or red: generally the smaller the variety the hotter they seem to be. Red chiles are usually sweeter and more mellow in flavor than the green ones; yellow chiles are similar in flavor to the red kind.

Dried chiles are ground to make hot red (cayenne) pepper and, combined with other spices, are used to make chili and curry powders. Chiles are also available canned in brine, and dried—whole or in flakes.

Buying & Storing
Bell peppers and chiles are available all year: select those that feel firm and have smooth glossy skins. They will keep well in the crisper drawer of the refrigerator up to one week.

Preparation
Cut off stalk ends of peppers and discard seeds and pith. Peppers for stuffing may be blanched in boiling water five minutes to make them pliable and reduce baking time.

To peel peppers, grill or bake whole until the skin blisters and blackens, then peel off the thin skin and discard. This also makes peppers more digestible.

Peppers may be sliced, diced or cut in larger pieces, as required. They are delicious sautéed, braised, stewed, steamed or baked.

When preparing chiles, take great care as the seeds and juices cause skin irritation. Wear rubber gloves when handling chiles and be sure not to touch your face or eyes during preparation. Cut off stalk end and split open pods. The tiny cream-colored seeds inside the pods are the hottest part and are usually removed before using: carefully scrape them out using a pointed knife and discard. Rinse pods very thoroughly under cold running water and pat dry. Chop finely or cut in thin slivers before using. When preparation is complete, wash hands, utensils and work surface thoroughly.

Serving Suggestions
Peppers are delicious eaten raw or cooked. Enjoy them crisp, juicy and raw in salads, or use as dipping sticks for hummus and taramasalata. Fill whole peppers with pâtés and cream cheese mixtures, then chill and slice in rings to serve as starters.

Use peppers in ratatouille and peperonata; add to soups, sauces and stir-fry dishes. Or use to add bite to pickles, chutney and relishes.

Chiles add pungency to many dishes, but remember that a little goes a long way. Steep a whole chile in a jar of oil and use the flavored oil in salad dressings, marinades and for sautéing. Add shredded chile to Chinese and Indian dishes, pizza toppings, omelets and scrambled eggs.

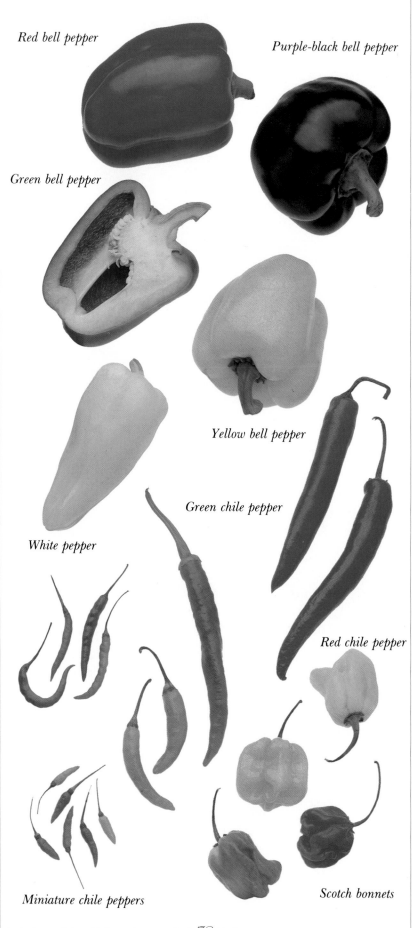

Red bell pepper

Purple-black bell pepper

Green bell pepper

Yellow bell pepper

Green chile pepper

White pepper

Red chile pepper

Miniature chile peppers

Scotch bonnets

Iced Avocado Soup

1 tablespoon sunflower oil
6 green onions, thinly sliced
4 teaspoons all-purpose flour
1-3/4 cups chicken stock
2 ripe avocados
2 teaspoons lemon juice
1-3/4 cups milk
2/3 cup dairy sour cream
Salt and white pepper to taste
2 good pinches red (cayenne) pepper
TO GARNISH:
Dairy sour cream
Chives

1. In a medium-size saucepan, heat oil. Add green onions and sauté 2 minutes, stirring frequently. Stir in flour and cook 1 minute, then gradually stir in stock and bring to a boil, stirring constantly. Reduce heat and simmer gently 10 minutes; cool.
2. Cut avocados in half, peel and remove seeds. Slice off a little for garnishing, brush with 1 teaspoon of lemon juice and set aside. Cut up remaining avocados. In a blender or food processor fitted with the metal blade, process avocados and cooled sauce mixture until smooth.
3. Add remaining lemon juice, milk and sour cream and blend thoroughly to combine. Season with salt and white pepper and red pepper and mix well. Chill at least 2 hours before serving.

Pour into 4 individual serving bowls and garnish each with sour cream, reserved slivers of avocado and a few chives.

Makes 4 servings.

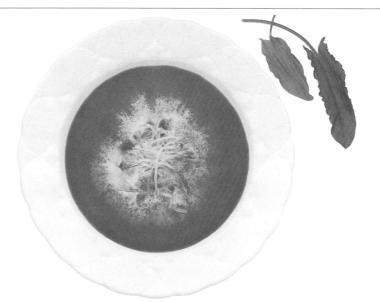

Nettle, Spinach & Sorrel Soup

3 ounces tender young nettle tops
Handful of small sorrel leaves
6 ounces spinach leaves
3 tablespoons butter
1 Spanish onion, thinly sliced
1 large potato, peeled and diced
1-3/4 cups chicken stock
1 cup milk
5 tablespoons half and half
Salt and pepper to taste
TO GARNISH:
Whipping cream
1/3 cup shredded Gruyère cheese (1-1/2 oz.)

1. Trim nettle tops and sorrel, removing sorrel stalks. Remove stalks from spinach. Rinse vegetables well in several changes of cold water. Shake well to drain, then shred coarsely.

2. In a large saucepan, melt butter, add shredded vegetables, onion and potato and fry gently 10 minutes, shaking pan frequently. Stir in stock and bring to a boil. Cover and simmer 20 minutes until potato and onion are tender.

3. Puree mixture in a blender or food processor fitted with the metal blade until smooth. Return to cleaned pan and stir in milk and half and half. Season with salt and pepper and reheat gently. Pour into 4 individual warmed soup bowls. Garnish with a swirl of whipping cream and sprinkle with grated cheese. Serve hot.

Makes 4 servings.

Note: Wear rubber gloves when preparing nettles.

Spiced Pumpkin Soup

1-1/2 pounds pumpkin
1 (1-inch) piece gingerroot
2 tablespoons butter
1 large Spanish onion, chopped
1/4 teaspoon garam masala
1 tablespoon all-purpose flour
2-1/2 cups chicken or vegetable stock
Salt and pepper to taste
1 tablespoon snipped chives
1 tablespoon chopped cilantro
1/4 cup half and half
TO GARNISH:
Sprigs of cilantro

1. Cut unpeeled pumpkin in even pieces; remove seeds. Place pumpkin in a steamer, cover and steam about 30 minutes or until tender. Cool slightly, then scrape away pulp from skin and mash well or puree in a blender or food processor fitted with the metal blade.

2. Peel gingerroot and chop very finely. In a large saucepan, melt butter. Add onion and fry gently 5 minutes. Stir in gingerroot and garam masala and cook 2 minutes, stirring constantly. Add flour and cook 1 minute. Gradually stir in stock and bring to a boil, stirring constantly. Reduce heat, then add pumpkin and season with salt and pepper.

3. Cover and simmer gently 10 minutes. Stir in herbs and half and half. Remove from heat and adjust seasoning, if necessary. Serve hot, garnished with cilantro sprigs.

Makes 4 to 6 servings.

Note: This soup is also good served garnished with toasted pumpkin seeds or finely shredded Cheddar cheese.

Fava Bean Soup Gratinée

1 tablespoon olive oil
3 tablespoons butter
1 garlic clove, crushed
1 Spanish onion, halved and sliced
3 large lettuce leaves, shredded
1 tablespoon all-purpose flour
2-1/2 cups chicken stock
1 pound shelled fava beans
Salt and pepper to taste
4 slices French bread, about 1 inch thick
1-1/2 teaspoons Dijon-style mustard
1 cup shredded Gruyère cheese (4 oz.)
TO GARNISH:
Snipped chives

1. In a large saucepan, heat oil and 2 tablespoons of butter. Add garlic, onion and lettuce and sauté 3 minutes, stirring frequently. Stir in flour and cook 1 minute. Stir in 1-1/4 cups of stock and bring to a boil, stirring frequently. Reduce heat and add fava beans. Cover and simmer 25 minutes.

2. In a blender or food processor fitted with the metal blade, process 1/2 of mixture until smooth; return to pan. Repeat with remaining mixture. Stir in remaining stock and season with salt and pepper. Reheat, stirring constantly, until piping hot. Transfer to 4 individual flameproof soup bowls and place on a broiler pan. Preheat broiler.

3. Spread French bread with remaining butter and mustard and press down into soup. Sprinkle with cheese and broil under preheated broiler 6 to 8 minutes, until golden and melted. Sprinkle with chives and serve immediately.

Makes 4 servings.

Note: For a chunky soup, puree 1/2 of mixture only in step 2. For a thinner soup, add a little extra stock.

Crudités with Skorthalia

3 slices day-old white bread, crusts removed
2 or 3 garlic cloves, crushed
1 tablespoon white wine vinegar
1/2 teaspoon each salt and pepper
1/3 cup olive oil
1 tablespoon lemon juice
1/4 cup ground almonds
1 tablespoon chopped fresh mint
1 head Belgian endive
1 red bell pepper
2 medium-size zucchini
2 stalks celery
12 radishes
1/4 head medium-size cauliflower
1 ripe olive, cut in slivers
Sprig of mint

1. Cut bread in cubes and place in a bowl. Add enough cold water to cover; soak 5 minutes. Spoon into a sieve and, using a wooden spoon, press bread against sieve to extract water. In a blender or food processor fitted with the metal blade, process bread, garlic, vinegar and salt and pepper until smooth.

2. With motor running, gradually add olive oil in a thin stream and blend until completely absorbed. Blend in lemon juice, ground almonds and chopped mint. Adjust seasoning, if necessary. Spoon into a serving bowl and chill at least 1 hour.

3. To prepare crudités, divide Belgian endive in separate leaves. Cut bell pepper in strips. Slice zucchini lengthwise, then cut in sticks. Cut celery in small sticks. Discard leaves from radishes and trim bottoms. Break cauliflower in bite-size flowerets. Wash all vegetables, drain and pat dry on paper towels. Chill until needed.

Place dip in center of a large serving platter. Arrange prepared vegetables in groups around bowl. Garnish dip with olives and mint.

Makes 4 to 6 servings.

Salmon & Guacamole Terrine

1 tablespoon butter
2 tablespoons all-purpose flour
1 (7-1/2-oz.) can salmon
5 teaspoons lemon juice
1-1/2 (1/4-oz.) envelopes unflavored gelatin (4-1/2 teaspoons)
5 tablespoons mayonnaise
4 teaspoons tomato paste
1/4 cup whipping cream
Few drops Worcestershire sauce
Salt and pepper to taste
2 ripe avocados
1 garlic clove, crushed
1 teaspoon olive oil
2 pinches red (cayenne) pepper
TO GARNISH:
Sprigs of dill

1. In a saucepan, melt butter, add flour and cook 1 minute. Drain salmon, reserving liquor; add enough water to measure 3/4 cup. Stir liquor into pan and bring to a boil, stirring; cook 2 minutes. Remove from heat. Flake salmon finely; stir into sauce.

In a bowl, mix 1 tablespoon lemon juice and 2 tablespoons water; sprinkle over gelatin and let stand 5 minutes. Set bowl in a pan of hot water; stir until dissolved. Let stand until cool but not set.

2. Add 1/4 cup of mayonnaise, tomato paste, cream and Worcestershire sauce to salmon mixture; season and mix well. Stir in gelatin; chill 15 min-

utes. Peel, seed and thinly slice 1 avocado; brush with 1 teaspoon of lemon juice. One-third fill a dampened 8" x 4" loaf pan with salmon mixture. Cover with 1/2 of avocado; repeat layers, finishing with salmon. Chill at least 2 hours.

3. Peel, seed and mash remaining avocado in a bowl. Add remaining lemon juice and mayonnaise, garlic, oil, red pepper and salt. Chill.

Dip terrine into very hot water 2 to 3 seconds, then turn out onto a serving plate. Swirl guacamole sauce over top. Garnish with dill.

Makes 6 to 8 servings.

Globe Artichokes à la Grecque

4 large globe artichokes
SAUCE:
2 tablespoons tomato paste
1/4 cup olive oil
2/3 cup dry white wine
2/3 cup water
1 small onion, finely chopped
1 garlic clove, crushed
1 teaspoon chopped oregano
2 sprigs of thyme
2 ripe tomatoes, peeled and chopped
Salt and pepper to taste
TO GARNISH:
Lemon wedges
Sprigs of oregano

1. Cut off stalks from artichokes and, using scissors, trim off pointed ends from outer leaves. Rinse well. Cook in boiling salted water 15 minutes. Drain well and stand upside down on paper towels to dry.

2. To prepare sauce, combine all ingredients in a saucepan. Mix well and bring to a boil. Cover and gently simmer gently 10 minutes, stirring occasionally. Remove thyme sprigs. Add artichokes to sauce, cover and cook gently 30 minutes. Carefully lift artichokes onto a plate and cool. Boil sauce, uncovered, 5 minutes; cool.

3. When artichokes are cold, remove chokes by spreading top leaves apart and pulling out inside leaves to reveal hairy choke. Using a teaspoon, scrape away hairs to expose heart. Arrange artichokes on 4 individual serving plates and spoon sauce around the artichokes. Cover and chill until needed.

Garnish with lemon wedges and oregano to serve.

Makes 4 servings.

Sesame-Glazed Asparagus

1 pound asparagus
4 tablespoons butter
6 green onions, thinly sliced diagonally
Finely grated peel of 1/2 small lemon
1 tablespoon lemon juice
Salt and pepper to taste
Pinch of red (cayenne) pepper
1 to 2 tablespoons sesame seeds, lightly toasted
1 teaspoon sesame oil
TO GARNISH:
Lemon slices
Sprigs of flat-leaf parsley

1. Cut off woody part at bottom of asparagus stems and, using a knife, scrape off white part of stems. Cut asparagus spears diagonally in 3 or 4 equal pieces. Place in a large sauce-pan and add enough boiling salted water to cover. Cook, covered, 8 to 10 minutes, until just tender, drain well.
2. In a large skillet, melt butter. Add green onions and sauté gently 1 min-ute. Add lemon peel and juice, then stir in asparagus. Toss lightly in sauce over low heat 2 to 3 minutes, until heated through.
3. Season with salt, pepper and red pepper. Turn onto a warmed serving platter and sprinkle with toasted sesame seeds and sesame oil. Garnish with lemon slices and parsley; serve hot.

Makes 4 servings.

Ham & Asparagus Bundles

16 asparagus spears
4 slices prosciutto, halved lengthwise
8 long chives
Lemon juice
Freshly ground black pepper
HOLLANDAISE SAUCE:
1/4 cup white wine vinegar
1 teaspoon black peppercorns
2 large egg yolks
8 tablespoons butter, room temperature
1 to 3 pinches red (cayenne) pepper
TO GARNISH:
Lemon twists

1. Cut off woody bottom of asparagus stems and, using a knife, scrape off white part of stems. Tie asparagus in bundles with heads together. Place in an asparagus steamer or saucepan and add enough boiling water to reach just below asparagus heads. Cover and boil 12 to 14 minutes or until tender. Lift asparagus from water, drain and set aside.

2. To prepare hollandaise sauce, place vinegar and peppercorns in a saucepan. Bring to a boil and boil until reduced by half. Place egg yolks in a bowl with 1 tablespoon of butter and beat well. Strain hot vinegar into egg yolks, beating well. Return to pan and place over very low heat. Gradu-

ally add remaining butter in small pieces, whisking constantly until sauce is thickened and smooth. (Keep removing pan from heat while whisking in butter to prevent curdling.) Add red pepper and pour into a serving dish.

3. Cut asparagus spears in half. Form 4 pieces in a stack, with spear ends on top. Wrap in a piece of prosciutto and tie with a chive. Repeat with remaining asparagus, prosciutto and chives. Sprinkle with lemon juice and pepper. Garnish with lemon twists and serve with Hollandaise sauce.

Makes 4 servings.

Filo-Wrapped Vegetables

3 green onions, finely chopped
1 cup finely chopped Chinese cabbage
1/2 red or green bell pepper, finely chopped
1 garlic clove, crushed
4 ounces peeled shrimp, thawed if frozen, chopped
1 tablespoon light soy sauce
1 tablespoon oyster sauce
1/2 teaspoon sugar
1 teaspoon cornstarch
4 sheets filo pastry
Vegetable oil for deep-frying
TO SERVE:
Green onion flowers, page 43
Chili sauce

1. In a small saucepan, mix green onions, Chinese cabbage, bell pepper, garlic and shrimp. Stir in soy sauce, oyster sauce, sugar and cornstarch. Cook over medium heat 3 minutes, stirring constantly. Remove from heat; set aside.

2. Cut sheets of filo pastry in 24 (5-inch) squares. Sandwich together in pairs to form 12 double-thickness squares. Place 1 teaspoon of prepared mixture in center of each square, then draw corners of pastry together. Twist and pinch firmly to seal.

3. Half-fill a large deep saucepan with oil and heat to 375F (190C) or until a cube of day-old bread browns in 40 seconds. Lower bundles into oil, a few at a time, and deep-fry 2 to 3 minutes, until golden-brown. Drain on paper towels and keep warm while cooking remainder. Arrange on a warm serving plate and garnish with green onion flowers. Serve hot with chili sauce for dipping.

Makes 4 to 6 servings.

Flounder & Watercress Bundles

2 flounder fillets, skinned and boned
1-1/2 bunches watercress
6 tablespoons butter
3 shallots, finely chopped
1 tablespoon fresh lime juice
Salt and pepper to taste
5 sheets filo pastry
TO SERVE:
Watercress sprigs
Lime twists
Tartar sauce

1. Preheat oven to 375F (190C). Cut flounder in thin strips and place in a bowl. Trim off watercress stalks and coarsely chop leaves. In a saucepan, melt 2 tablespoons of butter. Add watercress and shallots and sauté 2 minutes; transfer to bowl. Add lime juice and season with salt and pepper. Mix well and set aside.

2. Melt remaining butter in a pan. Cut filo sheets in half crosswise; brush lightly with butter. Fold each piece in 3 layers by folding top one-third section over center one-third and bottom one-third over top to form a long narrow strip. Brush lightly with but-

ter. Divide filling in 10 portions; place one in a corner of each pastry strip.

3. Fold pastry and filling over at right angles to form a triangle. Continue folding in this way along strip of pastry to form triangles. Brush all over with remaining melted butter and place on a baking sheet. Bake in preheated oven 15 minutes, until golden-brown and cooked through.

Serve hot, garnished with watercress sprigs and lime twists. Accompany with tartar sauce.

Makes 10 bundles.

Japanese-Style Cucumber

1 large cucumber
1 bunch watercress, stalks trimmed
4 ounces white crabmeat, thawed if frozen
1 (1-inch) piece gingerroot, peeled and grated
Salt and pepper to taste
SAUCE:
2 tablespoons rice vinegar
2 tablespoons chicken stock
2 teaspoons sugar
2 teaspoons Japanese soy sauce
TO GARNISH:
Watercress sprigs

1. Trim ends of cucumber, then slit lengthwise along one side through to center, taking care not to cut through. Using a teaspoon, very carefully remove seedy flesh from center to form a channel.

Blanch watercress in boiling water 30 seconds; drain well and pat dry on paper towels.

2. In a bowl, finely flake crabmeat; add gingerroot and season with salt and pepper. Hold cut edges of cucumber open and carefully insert crab mixture into channel; top with blanched watercress. Press cucumber edges together and wrap tightly in plastic wrap. Chill at least 2 hours.

3. To prepare sauce, combine all ingredients in a small saucepan and bring to a boil, stirring constantly. Remove from heat and cool.

Just before serving, cut cucumber in 3/4-inch-thick slices and arrange on a flat serving platter. Pour a small amount of sauce over each slice and garnish with watercress.

Makes 4 to 6 servings.

Spinach & Anchovy Soufflé

1 pound spinach, washed
4 tablespoons butter
1/2 cup all-purpose flour
1-1/4 cups milk
3 large egg yolks
1/2 cup shredded Cheddar cheese (2 oz.)
5 canned anchovy fillets, drained and finely chopped
Pepper to taste
Freshly grated nutmeg
4 large egg whites
TO GARNISH:
Cherry tomatoes

1. Discard tough stalks from spinach; shake off excess moisture. Pack into a saucepan (without additional water), cover and cook gently, turning occasionally, until volume decreases. Simmer 8 to 10 minutes, until tender. Place in a sieve and press with a saucer to extract moisture. Chop finely in a food processor.
2. Preheat oven to 350F (175C). Lightly grease a 5-cup soufflé dish. In a saucepan, melt butter, stir in flour and cook 1 minute. Add milk and bring to a boil, stirring constantly. Reduce heat and simmer 2 minutes, stirring constantly. Remove from heat and mix in spinach, egg yolks, cheese and anchovies. Season with pepper and nutmeg. Whisk egg whites until soft peaks form. Add 3 tablespoons to spinach mixture and stir to mix. Using a large metal spoon, lightly fold in remaining egg whites.
3. Pour mixture into prepared soufflé dish and smooth surface. Run back of a metal spoon around outer edge to form a central dome for a top hat effect. Bake in preheated oven 40 to 45 minutes, until well risen and golden-brown. Serve immediately, garnished with cherry tomatoes.

Makes 3 to 4 servings.

Chicken Szechuan

1 pound skinned chicken breast fillets
4 carrots
1 large red bell pepper, cored and seeded
6 green onions
1(1-1/2-inch) piece gingerroot
2 large eggs, beaten
Salt and pepper to taste
1 cup cornstarch
Vegetable oil for frying
1 garlic clove, crushed
4 teaspoons sugar
2 tablespoons soy sauce
2 tablespoons malt vinegar
TO GARNISH:
Sprigs of chervil

1. Slice chicken in thin strips. Cut carrots and bell pepper in matchstick strips. Cut green onions in slivers. Peel gingerroot and cut in slivers.

In a bowl, mix eggs with salt and pepper. Dip chicken strips into eggs, then into cornstarch to coat.
2. In a large saucepan, heat 2 inches of oil. Add 1/4 of chicken strips and fry 3 to 4 minutes, until cooked through and lightly golden. Drain on paper towels while cooking remainder in batches.

In a wok or skillet, heat 3 tablespoons oil. Add carrot and bell pepper strips and stir-fry 1-1/2 minutes.

Remove with a slotted spoon and set aside. Add garlic and gingerroot to pan and stir-fry 30 seconds.
3. Add sugar, soy sauce and vinegar to wok. Add vegetables and chicken and toss in sauce 2 to 3 minutes to heat through and glaze. Add green onion slivers and toss lightly. Serve immediately, garnished with chervil.

Makes 4 servings.

Note: This dish is delicious served with rice and accompanied by shrimp crackers.

Scampi Mediterranean

4 ripe tomatoes
1 Spanish onion
2 medium-size zucchini
1 red bell pepper, cored and seeded
1/4 cup olive oil
1 garlic clove, crushed
2 tablespoons all-purpose flour
1/4 cup dry white wine
1 tablespoon tomato paste
1 cup water
Salt and pepper to taste
1 pound uncooked peeled shrimp
3/4 cup fresh white bread crumbs
1 tablespoon chopped fresh marjoram
4 ounces mozzarella cheese
TO GARNISH:
Sprigs of marjoram

1. Preheat oven to 375F (190C). Place tomatoes in a large bowl, cover with boiling water and let stand 30 seconds. Drain and peel, then chop coarsely. Quarter and thinly slice onion. Cut zucchini in 1/4-inch slices. Cut bell pepper in thin strips.

In a large saucepan, heat 3 tablespoons of oil. Add onion, zucchini, bell pepper and garlic and cook gently 3 minutes.

2. Stir in flour and cook 1 minute. Add wine, tomato paste and water. Season with salt and pepper and cook gently 5 minutes, stirring occasionally. Add tomatoes and mix well. Divide mixture between 4 individual ovenproof dishes. Top with shrimp.

3. Heat remaining oil in a saucepan. Remove from heat and stir in bread crumbs and marjoram; mix well. Sprinkle over mixture in dishes. Chop mozzarella cheese and sprinkle on top. Bake in preheated oven 30 minutes or until topping is golden and shrimp is cooked. Serve hot, garnished with sprigs of marjoram.

Makes 4 servings.

Tempura

1 zucchini
1 small eggplant
1 green bell pepper, cored and seeded
8 button mushrooms
2 small sweet potatoes, peeled
6 green onions
2 lemon sole or flounder fillets, skinned and boned
4 cooked jumbo shrimp in shell
1 egg yolk
2 cups all-purpose flour
1/2 teaspoon baking soda
Vegetable oil for deep-frying
DIPPING SAUCE:
1 tablespoon mirin (Japanese rice wine)
1 tablespoon Japanese soy sauce
1-1/4 cups chicken stock

1. Cut zucchini and eggplant in 1/2-inch slices. Halve eggplant slices. Cut bell pepper in 1-inch pieces. Trim mushrooms. Cut sweet potatoes in 1/4-inch slices. Cut green onions and fish in bite-size pieces.

2. Peel shrimp, except for last section of tail shells.

To prepare batter, mix egg yolk and 1-3/4 cups ice cold water in a bowl. Sift flour and baking soda into another bowl and gradually add liquid, whisking until smooth. Let stand 15 minutes.

To prepare dipping sauce, combine mirin, soy sauce and stock in a saucepan and bring to a boil; cool.

3. Half-fill a wok or deep saucepan with vegetable oil and heat to 375F (190C) or until a cube of day-old bread browns in 40 seconds. Dip pieces of vegetable and fish, a few at a time, into batter. Deep-fry 1 to 2 minutes, until lightly golden. Drain well and keep warm while cooking remaining pieces.

Place a bowl of dipping sauce on each warmed serving plate and surround with vegetables and fish.

Makes 4 servings.

Eastern-Style Hotpot

7-1/2 cups chicken stock
1 (1-inch) piece gingerroot, peeled and grated
1 garlic clove, crushed
1 skinned chicken breast fillet
6 ounces beef fillet
2 ounces snow peas
2 medium-size zucchini
1/2 Chinese cabbage
1 bunch green onions
DIPPING SAUCE:
1/2 teaspoon chili sauce
1 garlic clove, crushed
1/4 cup light soy sauce
2 tablespoons peanut oil
Good pinch of sugar
1 teaspoon cider vinegar

1. In a large saucepan, combine stock, gingerroot and garlic. Cover and simmer 10 minutes. Meanwhile, cut chicken and beef in very thin strips.

2. Trim snow peas and remove strings. Slice zucchini thinly. Cut Chinese cabbage and green onions in short lengths. Arrange vegetables, chicken and steak on a platter.

To prepare dipping sauce, combine all ingredients. Pour into small serving bowls.

Transfer stock mixture to a Mongolian hotpot or large metal fondue pot over a burner in center of table; bring back to simmering.

3. Invite guests to cook their own meal. Place pieces of chicken or beef and 1 or 2 vegetables in small Chinese wire baskets and lower into simmering stock 1-1/2 to 2 minutes. Or hold food with wooden chopsticks in stock. Dip into dipping sauce before eating. Continue until ingredients are used. Serve remaining stock in soup bowls.

Makes 4 servings.

Stuffed Turnips

8 (4-oz.) turnips, peeled
10 tablespoons butter
1 onion, finely chopped
12 ounces veal scallops, minced
Finely grated peel of 1 large lemon
2 cups fresh bread crumbs
8 fresh sage leaves, finely chopped
1/4 cup chopped parsley
1 large egg, beaten
Salt and pepper to taste
1-1/4 cups chicken stock
1/2 cups whipping cream
8 slices large tomato, about 1/2 inch thick
TO GARNISH:
Sprigs of parsley and sage

1. In a saucepan of boiling salted water, cook turnips 15 to 20 minutes or until tender when pierced with a skewer. Drain and cool enough to handle. Hollow out turnips, using a melon baller or teaspoon, leaving 1/4-inch shells.

2. Preheat oven to 350F (175C). In a skillet, melt 8 tablespoons of butter. Add onion and veal and cook 5 minutes, stirring constantly. Remove from heat. Stir in lemon peel, bread crumbs, 1/2 of sage and parsley, beaten egg and salt and pepper; mix well. Spoon into hollowed-out turnips to cover top surface area completely; press in mounds. Place in a greased shallow ovenproof dish. Melt remaining butter and brush over stuffing and turnips. Add 1/2 cup of stock to dish. Bake in preheated oven 40 minutes, until stuffing is golden. Transfer turnips to a plate; keep warm.

3. Pour juices from dish into a pan. Add remaining stock and herbs and cream. Simmer 4 to 5 minutes, until slightly thickened. Place tomato slices on a warmed serving dish. Set a halved turnip on each and spoon sauce over turnip. Garnish with parsley and sage to serve.

Makes 4 servings.

Chillied Pork Chayotes

4 large chayotes
2 tablespoons olive oil
1 onion, chopped
1 garlic clove, crushed
8 ounces lean pork, minced
1 fresh green chile, seeded and finely chopped
4 tomatoes, peeled and chopped
2 tablespoons tomato paste
1 teaspoon cumin seeds
1 teaspoon hot chili powder
1/4 cup cold water
3/4 cup shredded Cheddar cheese (3 oz.)
4 bread sticks, crushed
TO GARNISH:
1/4 cup dairy sour cream
Sprigs of thyme
4 pickled chiles, if desired

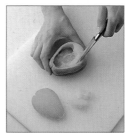

1. Cook chayotes in boiling salted water 30 minutes or until tender (test by inserting a skewer through skins). Drain and cool under running water. Set aside.

Preheat oven to 375F (190C). In a saucepan, heat oil. Add onion, garlic, pork and chile and fry gently 5 minutes, stirring frequently. Stir in tomatoes, tomato paste, cumin, chili powder and cold water. Cover and cook gently 5 minutes. Uncover and cook 5 minutes, until thickened.

2. Cut a sliver off 1 long side of each chayote to sit level. Slice off top 1/3 of each; cut out pulp and seeds, leaving a 1/4-inch border. Drain upside down on paper towels. Drain and chop pulp and seeds. Add to pork mixture with 1/2 of cheese and crushed bread sticks; mix well.

3. Spoon mixture into prepared chayote shells, piling it on top. Place in a greased shallow ovenproof dish. Mix remaining cheese and bread sticks and sprinkle over each one. Bake in preheated oven 25 minutes, until golden-brown. Top with sour cream and garnish with thyme and chiles, if desired.

Makes 4 servings.

Red Cabbage & Sausage

1 pound red cabbage
6 tablespoons butter
1 large Spanish onion, chopped
1 garlic clove, crushed
2 tablespoons light-brown sugar
2 tablespoons cider or wine vinegar
1-1/4 cups chicken stock
Salt and pepper to taste
1/4 to 1/2 teaspoon caraway seeds, if desired
4 frankfurters
4 ounces each chorizo and Zywiecka sausage
1 large baking apple
1-1/2 pounds new potatoes, cut in even pieces
TO GARNISH:
Watercress sprigs
Apple slices

1. Preheat oven to 300F (150C). Cut cabbage in quarters, dicarding stalk; shred finely. Heat 4 tablespoons of butter in a flameproof, enamel-lined casserole dish. Add onion, garlic and sugar and cook gently 5 minutes. Add cabbage and cook 5 minutes, stirring frequently. Add vinegar, stock, seasoning, and caraway seeds,if desired. Stir well, cover and bake in preheated oven 1-1/4 hours.

2. Meanwhile, cut frankfurters, chorizo and Zywiecka sausages in chunky slices. Peel, core and chop apple. Add sausages and apple to casserole, stir well. Cover and bake 30 minutes more.

3. Meanwhile, cook potatoes in boiling salted water 15 to 20 minutes, until tender. Drain, return to pan and place over a low heat a few seconds to dry. Mash with remaining butter and season; beat until smooth. Using a pastry bag fitted with a large star nozzle, pipe borders of mashed potatoes around edge of 4 individual serving dishes. Spoon cabbage mixture into center. Garnish with watercress and apple to serve.

Makes 4 servings.

Note: Zwyiecka is a smoked garlic spiced sausage available from delicatessens and supermarkets.

Fennel Italiano

4 large fennel bulbs
2 tablespoons olive oil
2 garlic cloves, chopped
1 large onion, quartered and thinly sliced
1 (14-1/2-oz.) can peeled tomatoes, chopped
2 tablespoons tomato paste
1/3 cup dry white wine or dry vermouth
Salt and pepper to taste
6 ounces mozzarella cheese, thinly sliced
2 to 3 teaspoons chopped marjoram
TO GARNISH:
Ripe olives

1. Preheat oven to 350F (175C). Cut off and reserve fennel leaves for garnish. Cut fennel bulbs in quarters. Cook in boiling salted water to cover 15 minutes; drain well.

2. Meanwhile in a large saucepan, heat oil. Add garlic and onion and sauté 5 minutes. Add tomatoes and juice, tomato paste and wine or vermouth. Season with salt and pepper. Bring to a boil. Simmer, uncovered, 10 minutes. In a blender or food processor fitted with the metal blade, process until smooth.

3. Arrange fennel in 4 greased individual ovenproof dishes. Pour sauce over fennel and cover with mozzarella cheese. Sprinkle with chopped marjoram and pepper. Bake in preheated oven 30 to 40 minutes or until fennel is tender. Garnish with olives and reserved fennel fronds. Serve hot.

Makes 4 servings.

Note: Serve with warm crusty bread.

Gruyère & Tomato Jalousie

1 tablespoon olive oil
2 medium-size zucchini, chopped
1 small onion, chopped
1 large tomato, chopped
2 teaspoons chopped fresh oregano
1 garlic clove, crushed
Salt and pepper to taste
1/2 cup shredded Gruyère cheese (2 oz.)
1/4 cup unsalted cashews, ground
1 (17-1/2-oz.) package frozen puff pastry, thawed
Beaten egg to glaze
TO GARNISH:
Sprigs of oregano

1. In a large saucepan, heat oil. Add zucchini and onion and fry 3 minutes. Remove from heat. Add tomato, oregano, garlic and seasoning. Cool in a strainer, then stir in cheese and ground nuts.

2. On a lightly floured surface, roll out pastry thinly to a 12-inch square. Mark in 2 pieces, one 12" x 6-1/2" and the other 12" x 5-1/2". Place smaller piece on a dampened baking sheet. Cover with zucchini mixture to within 1/2-inch of edges. Brush border with beaten egg.

Sprinkle other pastry lightly with flour, then fold in half lengthwise. Lightly mark a margin about 3/4 inch from the 3 cut edges. Using a sharp knife, cut folded edge at 1/4-inch intervals within marked margin.

3. Lift pastry over 1/2 of filling; unfold to cover remaining area. Seal edges, then press together and flute. Chill 30 minutes. Preheat oven to 425F (220C).

Brush jalousie lightly with beaten egg. Bake in preheated oven 15 minutes. Reduce heat to 375F (190C) and bake 15 minutes more, until golden. Serve hot or cold, garnished with oregano sprigs.

Makes 4 to 6 servings.

Pepper Rings

2/3 cup green lentils
1 onion, chopped
2 garlic cloves, chopped
2 dried red chiles, chopped
1/4 teaspoon ground coriander
1/4 teaspoon ground cumin
4 ounces shelled fava beans
2 tablespoons olive oil
1 tablespoon lemon juice
Salt and pepper to taste
1 each large red and green bell pepper
4 ounces goat cheese
TO GARNISH:
Sprigs of flat-leaf parsley

1. Place lentils in a bowl. Cover with boiling water and soak 30 minutes. Drain and place in a saucepan with 1 cup cold water. Add onion, garlic, chiles, coriander and cumin. Bring to a boil. Cover and simmer about 45 minutes, until water is absorbed and lentils are tender.

2. Meanwhile, cook fava beans in boiling water 15 to 20 minutes, until tender; drain. Place lentil mixture in a blender or food processor. Add fava beans, 4 teaspoons of oil, lemon juice and salt and pepper. Blend until fairly smooth; cool. Cut stalk ends off bell peppers and remove core and seeds.

Press bean mixture into bell peppers and level surfaces. Wrap in plastic wrap and chill at least 2 hours.

3. Preheat broiler. Cut bell peppers in 1/2-inch thick slices. Place on a broiler pan and brush lightly with remaining oil.

Slice cheese thinly and cut in quarters. Arrange 2 overlapping pieces on each bell pepper slice. Broil 4 to 5 minutes or until cheese is lightly golden. Serve immediately, garnished with parsley.

Makes 6 servings.

Tofu & Corn Stir-Fry

1 large red or green bell pepper, cored and seeded
1 bunch green onions
3 ounces button mushrooms
8 ounces tofu
3 tablespoons corn oil
16 dwarf (baby) ears-of-corn
4 ounces snow peas, trimmed
1 garlic clove, crushed
2 teaspoons light soy sauce
1 teaspoon dry sherry
1 (1/2-inch) piece gingerroot,
peeled and cut in thin slivers
1 teaspoon sugar
1/4 cup pine nuts, toasted

1. Cut bell pepper in thin slivers. Cut green onions diagonally. Slice mushrooms. Drain and cut tofu in cubes.
2. In a wok or large skillet, heat oil. Add corn and bell pepper and stir-fry 4 minutes. Add snow peas, green onions, mushrooms, tofu and garlic and stir-fry 4 to 5 minutes.
3. In a small bowl, mix soy sauce, sherry, gingerroot and sugar. Stir mixture into vegetables and heat through 1 minute, stirring gently. Spoon mixture into a warmed serving dish. Sprinkle with pine nuts and serve immediately.

Makes 4 servings.

Note: This dish is good served with rice or noodles.

Ratatouille Cheese Gougère

CHOUX PASTRY:
3-1/2 tablespoons butter
2/3 cup water
2/3 cup all-purpose flour, sifted
2 eggs, beaten
1/2 cup shredded Monterey Jack cheese (2 oz.)
FILLING:
1 small eggplant
1 large zucchini
Salt
3 tablespoons olive oil
2 red bell peppers, cored, seeded and cut in 1-inch pieces
1 Spanish onion, quartered and sliced
1 garlic clove, crushed
1 large tomato, peeled and chopped
Salt and pepper to taste

1. To prepare filling, quarter eggplant. Cut zucchini in 1/4-inch slices. Arrange in a colander, sprinkling each layer with salt. Let stand 30 minutes to drain.

2. Preheat oven to 400F (205C). To prepare pastry, in a saucepan, place butter and water. Heat gently until butter is melted. Bring to a boil, remove from heat and immediately add flour, all at once, and a pinch of salt, stirring quickly with a wooden spoon until smooth. Return pan to heat a few seconds and beat until mixture forms a ball and leaves side of pan clean. Remove from heat and gradually add eggs, beating after each addition until glossy. Stir in cheese. Spoon mixture around edge of 4 greased individual ovenproof dishes. Bake in preheated oven 30 minutes, or until well risen and golden.

3. Meanwhile, rinse eggplant and zucchini; drain and pat dry. In a pan, heat oil. Add all filling ingredients. Cover and cook gently 30 minutes. Spoon ratatouille into center of choux rings and serve immediately.

Makes 4 servings.

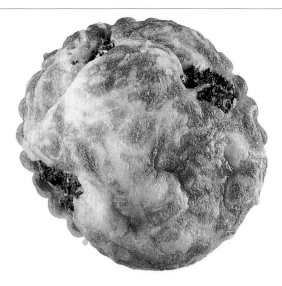

Broccoli Soufflé Tartlets

PASTRY:
1-1/2 cups all-purpose flour, sifted
1/2 cup whole-wheat flour
Pinch of salt
4 tablespoons margarine, chilled and diced
1/4 cup shortening, chilled and diced
1-1/4 cups finely shredded Cheddar cheese (5 oz.)
FILLING & TOPPING:
12 ounces broccoli spears, cut in even-sized spears
4 tablespoons butter
1/4 cup all-purpose flour
1-1/4 cups milk
2 eggs, separated
Salt and pepper to taste

1. Preheat oven to 400F (205C). To prepare pastry, place flour and salt in a bowl and cut in fats. Add 1/2 cup of cheese and mix well. Stir in 3 to 4 tablespoons cold water and mix to a firm dough. Knead gently and divide in 6 pieces. On a lightly floured surface, roll out dough and line 6 (4-inch) fluted flan pans. Prick bottoms with a fork. Line with foil and fill with dried beans. Bake 5 minutes; remove foil and beans and bake 5 minutes more. Remove from oven. Reduce heat to 375F (190C).

2. Cook broccoli in boiling salted water 6 to 8 minutes. Drain and cut in pieces. In a pan, melt butter. Stir in flour and cook 1 minute. Blend in milk. Bring to a boil, stirring. Cook 2 minutes.

3. Arrange 1/2 of broccoli in pastry shells. In a blender or food processor fitted with the metal blade, process remaining broccoli with sauce, egg yolks and 1/2 cup of remaining cheese. Season and transfer to a bowl. Whisk egg whites stiffly, then lightly fold into sauce. Spoon over broccoli and sprinkle with remaining cheese. Bake in oven 20 minutes, until golden. Serve hot.

Makes 6 servings.

Spinach & Ricotta Roulade

1-1/2 pounds spinach
2 tablespoons butter
3 shallots, very finely chopped
1/3 cup all-purpose flour
2/3 cup milk
2 tablespoons grated Parmesan cheese
4 large eggs, separated
Salt and pepper to taste
FILLING:
2 tablespoons dairy sour cream
1 cup ricotta cheese
3 green onions, chopped
2 tablespoons chopped fresh parsley
2 to 3 pinches red (cayenne) pepper
TO GARNISH:
Radish roses, page 115

1. Lightly grease a jellyroll pan and line with lightly greased parchment paper. Preheat oven to 400F (205C).

Prepare and cook spinach as for Spinach & Anchovy Soufflé, page 86. In a saucepan, melt butter. Add shallots and sauté 3 minutes. Stir in flour and cook 1 minute, then gradually blend in milk. Bring to a boil, then cook 2 minutes, stirring constantly (the sauce will be very thick). Remove from heat and stir in spinach, Parmesan cheese and egg yolks. Add salt and pepper and beat well.

2. Whisk egg whites until stiff but not dry; using a metal spoon, lightly fold into mixture. Spread into prepared pan. Level surface and bake in preheated oven 25 minutes or until set and firm to the touch.

Meanwhile, in a bowl, mix all filling ingredients; season with salt.

3. Turn roulade onto a sheet of lightly greased parchment paper. Loosen edges from lining paper and remove it in strips. Spread roulade with filling. Roll up, starting from a short side and using paper to help. Serve hot, garnished with radish roses.

Makes 6 servings.

Sorrel & Asparagus Crepes

24 young tender sorrel leaves
1/4 bunch watercress
4 tablespoons unsalted butter
1-1/4 cups all-purpose flour
Pinch of salt
2 eggs, beaten
1 cup milk
2/3 cup water
1 to 2 tablespoons corn oil
1 pound asparagus spears
2 tablespoons lemon juice
3/4 cup plain yogurt
Salt and pepper to taste
2 tomatoes, sliced
1/2 cup shredded Emmenthaler cheese (2 oz.)
TO GARNISH:
Lemon wedges

1. Shred sorrel. Chop watercress. In a saucepan, melt 1 tablespoon of butter. Add sorrel and watercress; cook gently 2 minutes; cool.

Sift flour and salt into a bowl. Add eggs and gradually beat in milk and water. Stir in sorrel and watercress.
2. In an 8-inch skillet, heat a little oil, swirling it over bottom and side. Pour in enough batter to coat bottom of pan evenly. Cook over high heat 2 minutes; turn and cook other side until golden; set aside. Use remaining batter to prepare 7 more crepes.
3. Preheat oven to 350F (175C). Prepare and cook asparagus as for Ham & Asparagus Bundles, page 82. Cut in bite-size pieces. Melt remaining butter in a pan; remove from heat. Add lemon juice, yogurt and salt and pepper. Spoon over crepes; fold each in half, then in half again. Insert asparagus into folds.

Arrange crepes in a greased shallow ovenproof dish. Place tomato slices between them and sprinkle with cheese. Cover with foil and bake in preheated oven 15 minutes. Uncover and bake 7 minutes more. Garnish with lemon wedges.

Makes 4 servings.

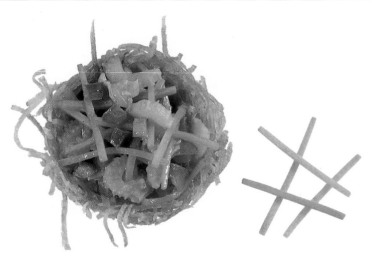

Stir-Fried Vegetable Nests

1 pound baking potatoes
1/2 teaspoon salt
1/2 cup plus 2 teaspoons cornstarch
Vegetable oil for deep-frying
1/4 Chinese cabbage
1 green bell pepper, cored and seeded
10 canned water chestnuts
5 stalks celery
3 carrots
1 fresh green chile
3 tablespoons peanut oil
1 garlic clove, crushed
1/4 cup water
3 tablespoons teriyaki sauce
2 tablespoons hoisin sauce

1. Finely grate potatoes into a colander; rinse well under cold running water. Drain well and thoroughly pat dry on paper towels. Place in a bowl. Add salt and 1/2 cup of cornstarch and mix well. Divide in 4 portions. Place 1 portion in a 4-inch metal sieve or basket. Spread potato to cover inside of sieve evenly. Place a slightly smaller sieve inside to keep shape during cooking.
2. Fill a wok or deep pan 2/3 full of vegetable oil and heat to 350F (175C). Lower sieve into hot oil and fry 4 minutes, until potato is golden; drain. Carefully loosen potato nest and keep warm. Cook remaining 3 nests in same way.
3. Shred cabbage. Dice bell pepper. Slice water chestnuts. Thinly slice celery. Peel and cut carrots in matchstick strips. Chop chile, discarding seeds. In a wok or skillet, heat peanut oil. Add garlic and vegetables; stir-fry 3 minutes.

Blend remaining cornstarch with water, teriyaki and hoisin sauces. Add to pan and cook 3 minutes, stirring constantly. Spoon into potato nests. Serve hot.

Makes 4 servings.

Scorzonera & Belgian Endive

8 ounces scorzonera or salsify
4 heads Belgian endive
1 tablespoon lemon juice
3 tablespoons butter
3 tablespoons all-purpose flour
2/3 cup milk
1/2 teaspoon Dijon-style mustard
1 to 2 tablespoons chopped fresh chervil
1 cup shredded Gruyère or Emmenthaler cheese (4 oz.)
Salt and pepper to taste
2 large slices cooked ham, halved
TO GARNISH:
3 small tomatoes
Sprigs of chervil

 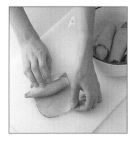 

1. Peel scorzonera and cut in 2-inch pieces. Place in a saucepan with whole Belgian endive, lemon juice and boiling water to cover. Simmer, covered, 10 minutes. Drain, reserving 1 cup liquor; set aside.
2. Preheat oven to 400F (205C). In a pan, melt butter. Stir in flour and cook 1 minute. Blend in milk and reserved liquor. Bring to a boil, stirring constantly. Simmer 2 minutes; stirring constantly. Remove from heat. Stir in mustard, chervil, 1/2 of cheese and salt and pepper.

Pat endive dry with paper towels.

Place scorzonera in 4 individual greased ovenproof dishes. Wrap endive in ham and place on top. Pour sauce over all and sprinkle with remaining cheese. Bake in preheated oven 25 minutes, until golden-brown.
3. To prepare tomatoes for garnish, insert a sharp pointed knife midway between stalk end and top of tomatoes. Cut all way around with a zigzag motion, through to center. Separate halves. Garnish dish with tomatoes and chervil.

Makes 4 servings.

Artichokes Dauphinoise

1-1/2 pounds Jerusalem artichokes
3 tablespoons butter
1 garlic clove, crushed
Salt and pepper to taste
2/3 cup half and half
2 tablespoons milk
1/2 cup shredded Gruyère cheese (2 oz.)
Freshly grated nutmeg
TO GARNISH:
Sprigs of sage

1. Scrub artichokes well in cold water, but do not peel. Parboil in boiling water to cover 8 to 10 minutes; drain well. Cool enough to handle, then peel and cut in thin slices.

2. Preheat oven to 350F (175C). Mix butter and garlic and use half to grease a 9-inch shallow ovenproof dish. Arrange 1/3 of artichoke slices in bottom of dish and season well with salt and pepper. Repeat layers, seasoning each layer.

3. In a small saucepan, heat half and half and milk until hot, but not boiling. Pour over artichokes. Sprinkle with cheese and nutmeg and dot with remaining garlic-flavored butter. Bake in preheated oven 45 minutes, until golden-brown. Serve hot, garnished with sage.

Makes 4 servings.

Variation: Use new potatoes when artichokes are unavailable—cooked this way they are extremely good.

Glazed Vegetables with Madeira

6 medium-size zucchini
1 pound carrots
4 tablespoons unsalted butter
1 teaspoon green peppercorns, coarsely crushed
Salt to taste
Finely grated peel and juice of 1 lime
2 or 3 teaspoons Madeira wine
Vegetable oil for deep-frying
TO GARNISH:
8 large sprigs of fresh parsley
Lime twists

1. Using a canelle knife, cut thin grooves down length of zucchini. Slice thinly and set aside. Peel carrots, slice thinly and cook in boiling salted water 3 minutes. Drain, refresh with cold water and drain again; set aside.

Rinse and dry parsley for garnish thoroughly on paper towels.

2. In a skillet, melt butter. Add zucchini and sauté 1 minute. Add carrots and cook 2 minutes, stirring frequently to glaze. Stir in crushed peppercorns, salt and lime peel and juice and heat through 1 minute. Transfer to a warmed serving dish. Add wine to pan, deglaze and pour over vegetables. Keep warm while preparing parsley for garnish.

3. Half-fill a deep saucepan with oil and heat to 365F (185C) or until a cube of day-old bread browns in 45 seconds. Place parsley sprigs in a frying basket and submerge into hot oil; cook a few seconds until sizzling stops. Drain briefly. Garnish vegetables with parlsey and lime twists.

Makes 4 to 6 servings.

French-Fried Celery Root

1 pound celery root
1 lemon slice
2 egg whites
2 cups fresh white bread crumbs
1/2 teaspoon dried mixed herbs
Vegetable oil for deep-frying
CHILI DIP:
2 tablespoons tomato paste
2 teaspoons chili sauce
1 garlic clove, crushed
1 teaspoon sesame oil
3 tablespoons water
6 tablespoons mayonnaise
1 teaspoon lemon juice
TO GARNISH:
Sprigs of flat-leaf parsley

1. Peel and cut celery root in quarters, then slice in 1/4-inch slices. Place in a pan of boiling salted water with lemon slice and cook 5 minutes. Drain, return to pan and shake over low heat a few seconds to dry; cool.
2. To prepare chili dip, in a saucepan, combine tomato paste, chili sauce, garlic, sesame oil and water; simmer 2 minutes. Cool, then mix with mayonnaise and lemon juice. Spoon into a small serving bowl and chill until needed.
3. In a bowl, lightly beat egg whites until slightly frothy. On a plate, mix bread crumbs with herbs. Dip slices of celery root into egg whites. Allow excess to drain, then coat in bread crumb mixture, pressing on firmly with fingers. Half-fill a deep pan with oil and heat to 375F (190C) or until a cube of day-old bread browns in 40 seconds. Lower celery root slices into hot oil, a few at a time. Deep-fry about 3 minutes, until golden-brown and crisp. Drain on paper towels and keep warm while frying remainder. Serve hot, garnished with parsley and accompanied by chili dip.

Makes 4 to 6 servings.

Spiced Broccoli & Cauliflower

8 ounces broccoli spears
1/2 cauliflower
4 cardamom pods
4 tablespoons butter
1 small onion, thinly sliced and separated in rings
1/2 teaspoon cumin seeds
1/4 teaspoon ground coriander
1 (1/2-inch) piece gingerroot, peeled and grated
1/4 to 1/2 teaspoon turmeric
1 garlic clove, if desired, crushed
2 teaspoons lemon juice
Salt to taste
Plain yogurt, if desired
TO GARNISH:
Sprigs of cilantro

1. Cut off broccoli flowerets and divide in even-size pieces. Cut stalks in half lengthwise, then cut in bite-size pieces. Divide cauliflower in even-size flowerets, discarding center stalk. Cook broccoli stalks in boiling salted water 3 minutes. Add cauliflower and broccoli flowerets and continue cooking 3 minutes until vegetables are barely tender; drain well.
2. Meanwhile, crush cardamom pods and remove seeds. In a large skillet, melt butter. Add onion, cumin seeds, coriander, gingerroot, cardamom, turmeric and garlic, if desired. Cook gently 5 minutes, stirring frequently. Add lemon juice and cook 3 minutes. Season with salt.
3. Add prepared broccoli and cauliflower to skillet. Toss gently in spiced butter and heat through 3 minutes, stirring gently. Spoon into a warmed serving dish. Drizzle with yogurt, if desired, and garnish with cilantro.

Makes 4 servings.

Fried Wild Rice & Vegetables

1/3 cup wild rice
2/3 cup Basmati rice
6 ounces bean sprouts
2 eggs
2 teaspoons water
Salt and pepper to taste
1-1/2 teaspoons butter
6 tablespoons corn oil
2 stalks celery, thinly sliced diagonally
1 leek, finely shredded
1 garlic clove, crushed
1 teaspoon sesame oil
2 to 3 teaspoons sake or dry sherry
1 to 2 tablespoons light soy sauce
6 cos or romaine lettuce leaves, finely shredded
Celery leaves to garnish

1. Rinse wild and Basmati rice separately under cold running water. Cook wild rice in boiling salted water 10 minutes. Add Basmati rice to pan and cook 20 minutes. Rinse and drain. Cool, then chill several hours or overnight.

Blanch bean sprouts in boiling water 30 seconds; drain.

2. Beat eggs with water and seasoning. In an 8-inch skillet, heat butter. Add eggs and cook until underside is golden and top is set. Turn out onto a flat surface; cool. Roll up, golden-side outside and slice thinly; set aside.

In a wok or skillet, heat 2 tablespoons of corn oil. Add celery, leek and garlic and stir-fry 2 minutes. Add bean sprouts and stir-fry 1 minute. Add 2 tablespoons corn oil, stir in rice and stir-fry 2 minutes.

3. Add sesame oil, sake or sherry and season; stir-fry 2 minutes. Spoon into a warmed serving dish; sprinkle with soy sauce. Heat remaining corn oil. Add lettuce and stir-fry about 2 minutes, until slightly wilted and glistening. Arrange around rice. Garnish with omelet slices and celery leaves.

Makes 4 servings.

Sweet Potato Marquise

2 pounds sweet potatoes, peeled
6 tablespoons butter
Salt and pepper to taste
2 or 3 pinches of ground mace
2 egg yolks
3 tablespoons slivered almonds
4 ounces fresh green beans
1 tablespoon corn oil
3 shallots, finely chopped
2 tomatoes, peeled and chopped
1/3 cup frozen petits pois or green peas
1/4 cup chicken stock
6 to 8 long chives
TO GARNISH:
Sprigs of flat-leaf parsley

1. Cut sweet potatoes in even pieces and cook in boiling salted water 15 to 20 minutes or until tender. Drain well, return to pan and shake over low heat a few seconds to dry off. Mash thoroughly. Add 4 tablespoons of butter and season with salt, pepper and mace. Stir in egg yolks and beat well.

2. Preheat oven to 400F (205C). Lightly grease a baking sheet. In a pastry bag fitted with a 1/2-inch plain nozzle, pipe 6 to 8 nests of potato mixture on baking sheet. Melt remaining butter and brush lightly over nests; stud with almonds. Bake on top shelf of preheated oven 15 to 20 minutes.

3. Meanwhile, trim green beans. Cut in half and cook in a steamer 8 to 10 minutes or until tender.

Meanwhile, in a saucepan, heat oil. Add shallots, tomatoes, petits pois and stock. Cover and cook gently 5 to 6 minutes. Season with salt and pepper and keep warm.

Transfer sweet potato mixture nests to a warmed serving plate and fill with vegetable mixture. Arrange bundles of beans attractively between nests. Garnish with parsley and serve hot.

Makes 6 to 8 servings.

Jansson's Temptation

1-1/2 pounds baking potatoes, peeled
4 tablespoons unsalted butter
1 large onion, quartered and thinly sliced
1/3 cup whipping cream
1/2 cup milk
1 (2-oz.) can anchovy fillets, drained
Salt and pepper to taste
6 tablespoons fresh white bread crumbs
TO GARNISH:
Sprigs of flat-leaf parsley

1. Preheat oven to 400F (205C). Cut potatoes in half lengthwise. Place flat-side down and cut in 1/8-inch slices, then cut slices in 1/4-inch matchstick strips. In a large skillet, melt 3 tablespoons of butter. Add onion and sauté gently 5 minutes, stirring occasionally.

2. Add potato sticks and continue frying gently 5 minutes, stirring frequently to prevent sticking. Remove from heat. Mix whipping cream and milk. Place 1/2 of onion and potato mixture in a shallow ovenproof dish. Chop 1/2 of anchovies and sprinkle over top. Season with salt and pep-

per. Pour 1/2 of cream mixture over top. Cover with remaining onion and potato mixture and press down firmly with a fish slice. Season again.

3. Sprinkle bread crumbs evenly over surface and press lightly. Pour remaining cream mixture over top. Melt remaining butter and drizzle over top. Bake in preheated oven 35 to 40 minutes, until golden-brown and cooked through. Cut remaining anchovies in half lengthwise and arrange in a lattice design over top. Garnish with parsley and serve hot.

Makes 4 servings.

Garlic-Baked Potatoes

1-1/2 pounds small even-size new potatoes
1 tablespoon corn oil
1 tablespoon butter
1 garlic clove, crushed
Salt and pepper to taste
2 sprigs of mint
4 bacon slices
4 green onions
TO GARNISH:
Sprigs of mint

1. Preheat oven to 350F (175C). Scrub potatoes well under cold water, but do not peel. Leave whole and pat dry on paper towels. Prick each potato twice with a fine skewer.
2. In a flameproof casserole dish, heat oil and butter. Add potatoes and fry 5 minutes to brown lightly, turning frequently. Stir in garlic and salt and pepper. Add 2 mint sprigs. Cover and bake in preheated oven 20 minutes or until almost tender.
3. Cut bacon in thin strips. Slice green onions diagonally in thin slivers. Remove mint from casserole and stir in bacon and green onions. Cook, uncovered, 10 minutes, until bacon is crisp and potatoes are tender. Spoon into a warmed serving dish and garnish with mint sprigs.

Makes 4 servings.

Variation: Use 3 or 4 shallots instead of green onions. Thinly slice and separate in rings.

Antipasto Salad

1 pound taro root
2 tablespoons snipped chives
1 tablespoon chopped fresh parsley
2 heads Belgian endive
1 large fennel bulb
1 green bell pepper, cored and seeded
1 large tomato
1/2 head chicory
1/2 ripe Ogen melon
DRESSING:
3 tablespoons walnut oil
3 tablespoons sunflower oil
2 tablespoons white wine vinegar or lemon juice
1 garlic clove, crushed
Salt and pepper to taste

1. Peel taro root. Cut in even-size pieces and cook in boiling salted water 10 to 15 minutes, until just tender; do not overcook. Drain and cool enough to handle. Dice and place in a bowl. In a small bowl, whisk all dressing ingredients. Pour 1/4 cup of dressing over warm taro root. Add herbs and mix gently to avoid breaking up taro root; cool.

2. Separate Belgian endive in leaves. Cut fennel in quarters and separate layers. Slice bell pepper in rings. Thinly slice tomato. Divide chicory in leaves. Cut melon in thin slices, dis-

card seeds, then cut pulp away from peel.

3. Arrange chicory on individual serving platters. Spoon taro root salad in center. Arrange other prepared vegetables and melon around salad. Whisk remaining dressing until thoroughly combined and drizzle over salad.

Makes 4 to 6 servings.

Variation: Use new potatoes or parboiled celery root instead of taro root.

Ribbon & Rose Salad

2 medium-size zucchini
2 large carrots
1 daikon
DRESSING:
2/3 cup mayonnaise
2 tablespoons snipped chives
1 garlic clove, crushed
1 tablespoon lemon juice
1 teaspoon tomato paste
1 tablespoon half and half
1/2 teaspoon sugar
Salt and pepper to taste
TO GARNISH:
12 small round radishes

1. Fill a large bowl of cold water with 24 ice cubes. Using a potato peeler, cut very thin lengthwise slices from zucchini. Drop into iced water. Peel carrots and daikon and drop into iced water.
2. To prepare radish roses for garnish, trim away root ends and larger leaves—leave on small leaves. Using a small sharp pointed knife, cut 3 petals from root to leaf end of radish, taking care not to cut through. Place in iced water. Push all vegetables down into water and refrigerate several hours to crisp and slightly curl ribbons and open roses.
3. To prepare dressing, combine all ingredients in a small bowl and mix well. Spoon into 4 small dishes and place on individual serving plates.

Drain vegetables and pat dry. Arrange ribbons of vegetables around bowls of dressing and garnish each salad with radish roses.

Makes 4 servings.

Spinach & Bacon Salad

8 ounces tender young spinach
8 bacon slices
2 slices white bread
2 shallots
1/2 cup olive oil
1 garlic clove, crushed
1/3 cup dark raisins
2 egg yolks
1/2 teaspoon dry mustard powder
4 anchovy fillets, mashed finely
2 tablespoons lemon juice
2 tablespoons grated Parmesan cheese
1 teaspoon sugar
Pepper to taste

1. Remove stalks from rinsed and dried spinach. Tear leaves in bite-size pieces and place in a serving bowl. Cut bacon in smaller pieces. Remove crusts and cut bread in cubes. Thinly slice shallots and separate in rings.
2. In a medium-size skillet, fry bacon until crisp and golden. Drain and cool. Mix oil with garlic and 2 tablespoons of bacon fat in skillet. Add bread cubes and fry until golden-brown, turning frequently. Drain and cool. Add bacon, raisins and shallots to spinach and mix lightly. Chill until needed.
3. In a small bowl, mix egg yolks, dry mustard, anchovies, lemon juice, Parmesan cheese and sugar. Season with pepper, then gradually whisk in remaining garlic-flavored oil in a thin stream, whisking well to yield a smooth sauce. Just before serving, add dressing to salad and toss lightly until all ingredients are evenly coated. Sprinkle croutons over salad and serve immediately.

Makes 4 servings.

Chicken & Shrimp Salad

8 ounces skinned chicken breast fillet
8 ounces peeled shrimp, thawed if frozen
2 teaspoons sesame oil
1 garlic clove, crushed
1 (1-inch) piece gingerroot, peeled and grated
3 tablespoons light soy sauce
4 small firm tomatoes
1/4 head Chinese cabbage
4 ounces bean sprouts
1/2 head lollo rosso
Generous handful lamb's lettuce
1 bunch watercress
2 tablespoons corn or peanut oil
1 onion, quartered and cut in thin slivers
2 teaspoons sugar

1. Cut chicken in fine slivers and place in a bowl. Add shrimp, then stir in sesame oil, garlic, gingerroot and soy sauce. Mix well and refrigerate 30 minutes.

2. Meanwhile, prepare tomato roses for garnish. Using a small sharp knife and starting at smooth end of each tomato, remove peel in an even continuous strip about 1/2 inch wide. Start to curl peel from bottom end, with pulp-side inside, to form a bud-shape. Continue winding peel around bud-shape to form a rose. Cover loosely with plastic wrap and chill until needed.

Finely shred Chinese cabbage.

Blanch bean sprouts in boiling water 15 seconds. Drain and refresh with cold water; drain again. Shred lollo rosso. Place prepared vegetables in a bowl and add lamb's lettuce and watercress, reserving a few sprigs for garnish. Toss well, then transfer salad to a shallow serving dish.

3. In a wok or skillet, heat oil. Add onion and stir-fry 2 minutes. Add shrimp mixture and stir-fry 3 to 4 minutes. Stir in sugar. Spoon hot mixture over salad. Garnish with tomato roses and watercress. Serve immediately.

Makes 4 servings.

Belgian Endive Salad

8 ounces fresh green beans, trimmed
2 heads Belgian endive, separated in leaves
1/2 head chicory, torn in bite-size pieces
1/2 cup pecan halves
1 green bell pepper, cored, seeded and sliced in rings
2 tomatoes, cut in wedges
5 ounces Roquefort cheese
ROQUEFORT DRESSING:
2 egg yolks
1 teaspoon sugar
1/2 teaspoon each salt and pepper
1/2 teaspoon Dijon-style mustard
2 tablespoons lemon juice or white wine vinegar
1-1/4 cups olive oil
2 tablespoons half and half
1 tablespoon snipped chives

1. Cook green beans in a little boiling salted water 6 to 8 minutes, until just tender. Drain and refresh under cold running water; drain again. Arrange Belgian endive in a border around a serving bowl. Fill center with chicory. Arrange pecans, bell pepper rings and tomato wedges on top, allowing chicory to show around edge as a border. Dice 3 ounces of Roquefort cheese and place in center of salad. Cover with plastic wrap and chill.
2. To prepare dressing, in a small bowl, combine egg yolks, sugar, salt, pepper and mustard and whisk well. Gradually blend in lemon juice or vinegar. Set bowl on a damp towel to keep it steady. Add oil, drop by drop, beating well after each addition, until about 1/4 of oil has been added. Gradually increase amount of oil being added to a thin steady stream and continue beating to a thick consistency.
3. Stir half and half into dressing. Finely crumble in remaining Roquefort and beat until smooth. Stir in chives and transfer to a serving bowl. Serve with salad.

Makes 4 servings.

Italian Salad Cups

1 green bell pepper
16 cherry tomatoes, halved
8 pitted ripe olives
8 stuffed green olives
4 green onions
4 ounces mozzarella cheese
1 head radicchio
DRESSING:
3 tablespoons olive oil
1 tablespoon red wine vinegar
1 garlic clove, crushed
Salt and pepper to taste
1/2 teaspoon wholegrain mustard
1/2 teaspoon sugar
TO GARNISH:
Sprigs of oregano

1. Skewer bell pepper firmly on a fork and hold over a flame until skin blisters and blackens. Or cut bell pepper in half and place skin-side up, on a broiler pan. Preheat broiler and broil bell pepper until skin blisters and blackens. Cool, then peel. Discard stalk end, core and seeds. Cut bell pepper in thin slivers and place in a bowl with cherry tomatoes.

2. Slice olives; thinly slice green onions. Cut cheese in small cubes. Add olives, green onions and cheese to bowl and toss gently.

Cut stem end off radicchio and carefully separate leaves. Select 8 cup-shaped leaves, rinse in cold water and pat dry. Wash and finely shred 4 more radicchio leaves and add to bowl.

3. Place all dressing ingredients in a screw-top jar and shake vigorously until well blended. Add to salad ingredients and toss lightly. Fill radicchio cups with salad mixture and arrange on a serving plate. Garnish with oregano.

Makes 4 servings.

Lettuce & Avocado Salad

2 heads cos or romaine lettuce
1 large ripe avocado
1 teaspoon lemon juice
DRESSING:
4 ounces raspberries
2 teaspoons sugar
5 teaspoons distilled malt vinegar
3 tablespoons sunflower oil
Salt and pepper to taste
TO GARNISH:
Chives

1. To prepare dressing, place 3 ounces of raspberries in a bowl; add sugar. Reserve remaining raspberries for garnish. Heat vinegar in a small saucepan until hot; pour over raspberries and cool. Strain through a fine sieve into a bowl, pressing raspberries with back of a wooden spoon to extract all juice and pulp. Add oil to raspberry mixture and season with salt and pepper. Whisk until blended.
2. Cut lettuce in quarters and arrange on a serving platter. Halve avocado, remove seed and peel. Cut pulp lengthwise in slices and brush with lemon juice.
3. Arrange avocado slices and lettuce on individual serving dishes. Just before serving, whisk dressing again and spoon a small amount over salad. Serve remainder separately. Garnish salad with remaining raspberries and chives.

Makes 4 servings.